don't jump!

don't jump!

The Northwest Winter Blues Survival Guide

Illustrations by
Alli Arnold

Novella Carpenter
and Traci Vogel

SASQUATCH BOOKS
SEATTLE

Published by Sasquatch Books
Distributed in Canada by Raincoast Books Ltd.
Printed in the United States of America

05 04 03 02 01 00 5 4 3 2 1

Cover and interior illustrations: Alli Arnold
Cover design: Karen Schober
Interior design and composition: Dan McComb and Karen Schober

Library of Congress Cataloging in Publication Data
Vogel, Traci.
Don't Jump! : the northwest winter blues survival guide / Traci Vogel and Novella Carpenter ; illustrated by Alli Arnold.
p. cm.
Includes bibliographical references.
ISBN 1-57061-266-8 (alk. paper)
1. Northwestern States--Climate--Physiological effect--Humor. 2. Northwestern States--Climate--psychological aspects--Humor. 3. Seasonal affective disorder--Northwestern States--Humor. 4. Winter--Northwestern States--Humor. I. Carpenter, Novella, 1972- II. Arnold, Alli. III. Title.
QP82.2.C5 V644 2000
613'.09795--dc21 00-029651

Sasquatch Books
615 Second Avenue
Seattle, Washington 98104
(206) 467-4300
www.SasquatchBooks.com
books@SasquatchBooks.com

Publisher's disclaimer: Please use common sense. No winter survival guide can act as a substitute for experience, careful planning, and appropriate training. There is inherent danger in all activities described in this book (especially the overeating chapter, but also the sex chapter, the part about taking excessive amounts of over-the-counters, the bikini exercises, and well, pretty much the whole thing), and readers must assume responsibility for their own winter actions, fashion, safety, and weight gain.

For all the folks who've suffered through the Northwest winter and stuck around for another, and then another, and another, and then another . . . Dear Lord, when will you learn?!

Contents

Acknowledgments

Alli Arnold, thank you for your illustrations and your profound respect for heshers. Props to my co-author and co-founder of BRITE who, when I was feeling down, would drive me to the liquor store. Big sloppy kisses for everyone at Sasquatch Books for their support. Thanks to all my friends who provided funny titles, tales of scotch-guard huffing, and disturbing insights into their bleak winters. Bill, hibermate Top #1, who joined me to consume enormous amounts of barbecue, chicken, donuts, and coffee throughout many a hard winter (without complaint!), I salute you. And, finally, Miss Piggy, if you're still out there, *Miss Piggy's Guide to Life* was and will continue to be the answer to all of the tough questions life throws my way; you are my inspiration.

–NC

Thanks to the inventor of the old lady plastic rain cap, whoever you are: you began my odyssey. Also, shout out to Mom and Dad, who taught me to jump in mud puddles. Alli Arnold, you color my dreams; and the ladies of ClitLit, you will always, somewhere in Seattle, be knitting waterproof protection in the form of cheap wine, great writing, and good old-fashioned girlfriend love.

–TV

Introduction

No, no, you're right—it doesn't get that cold here during the winter. And it rains more in New York City or Atlanta, Georgia, than in Portland or Seattle or Vancouver.

But you know what? The Northwest winter still sucks. It's dark. It's damp. You grow fat in a carbohydrate feeding frenzy. You want to sleep all day and all night. You lose your sex drive (no, anything but that!). Then there's that moment in January when you realize that the puddle in the driveway eerily reflects your soul. Maybe you should end . . . it . . . all . . .

But wait! Before you creep out onto a building's ledge, or hurl your body off a bridge, please consider the wise words of the Beyond Rain and Ignorance Teaching Establishment (BRITE) instead.

BRITE came into being during the really bad winter of 1995/96 to study the intricate effects of a really bad winter on the general populace. That first year, we discovered not only that hibernation has not evolved out of the human species, but also that wet hair tends to make most people look like drowned rats (and emits strange odors). Our group then moved toward studying recovered winter memories, the social implications of people who wear hats versus people who use umbrellas, and the real reason raindrops seem able to penetrate that one vulnerable spot where your collar meets the back of your neck. BRITE also unearthed data that proved Northwest residents have a tendency to internalize weather. This can result in mood swings, seasonally affecting every area of their lives, including really important areas like fashion (Winter: Big gray coat. Summer: Adorable pink gingham shorts, cropped white cotton tank top, and that straw hat! The cutest!), nourishment (Winter: Beef jerky *is* delicious on cheesecake. Summer: I crave . . . bean sprouts!), and fun (Winter: Let's rest by the fire. Summer: Let's join the circus, start our own country, and erect a log cabin in the backyard!).

And so now, after years of conducting cutting-edge scientific research, we proudly present to you the collected wisdom of BRITE in *Don't Jump! The Northwest Winter Blues Survival Guide.* You can fight climate determinacy, and *Don't Jump!* is your handbook for surviving that battle. Learn how the whipped cream on your mocha can forecast the weather; follow our suggestions for creating a dating strategy that will land you the ultimate hibermate; and discover how to emerge from your long winter with grace, and more importantly, without scaring others. With these tips and more, we hope you will find this seasonal guide useful, and if not—why not use the book to cover your head during a sudden squall?

—Novella Carpenter and Traci Vogel, BRITE founders

Is this you?

Are You a Prisoner

POW

❶ **Just as you are about to go out on the town, it starts raining. You:**

Ⓐ Wrap your entire body in Saran Wrap before going out, hell-bent for fun.

Ⓑ Cancel your plans to go out, relax, and read a book instead.

Ⓒ Slice open your wrists.

❷ **SAD stands for:**

Ⓐ Seasonal Affective Disorder.

Ⓑ Satanic Acrobats on Drugs.

Ⓒ How you feel all the time during the winter.

❸ **A light box is:**

Ⓐ A device used to administer full-spectrum light to people who have SAD.

Ⓑ That thing in E.T.'s chest that Neil Diamond sings about.

Ⓒ A synonym for matches, useful for the pack a day you smoke during the winter.

❹ **Winter blues are:**

Ⓐ Feelings of mild depression during the winter caused by lack of light.

Ⓑ B. B. King in December.

Ⓒ The color of your feet.

❺ **When the weatherforecaster predicts rain turning to showers, you:**

Ⓐ Don the hip waders, drink five cups of black coffee, and bring extra socks to work.

Ⓑ Sigh and pack an umbrella.

Ⓒ Call in sick and make crank phone calls to the television studio, repeatedly asking what exactly is the difference between rain and showers.

of Weather (POW)?

❻ Global warming will affect the Northwest by:

Ⓐ Causing more rain in the winter, reduced snowpacks, and lower river flows.

Ⓑ Increasing the length of summer, you hope.

Ⓒ You don't care if California bursts into flames as long as it gets warmer here.

❼ Sunscreen is:

Ⓐ A substance used to protect the skin cells from ultraviolet (UV) light.

Ⓑ A substance used by people in faraway places to ward off sunburn.

Ⓒ A mythical substance.

❽ The best thing about dark winter nights is:

Ⓐ Lots of casual sex.

Ⓑ You can get more reading done.

Ⓒ Neighbors don't notice your self-inflicted whippings near the window.

❾ Daylight Saving Time was invented to:

Ⓐ Increase morning daylight hours during winter.

Ⓑ Cause you to go to sleep at 6:30 p.m. every night.

Ⓒ Crush what little will you have left to live.

❿ Your body needs more food during the winter because:

Ⓐ Your body requires more energy to keep warm.

Ⓑ It's the holiday season.

Ⓒ Your size 16 winter wardrobe won't fit otherwise.

⓫ If you get a cold during the winter:

Ⓐ Take zinc, echinacea, and vitamin C; drink liquids; and get lots of rest.

Ⓑ Take some over-the-counters.

Ⓒ Go back to your hometown and live with your mother.

⓬ Your three favorite drinks during the winter are:

Ⓐ Vodka gimlet, Greyhound, and coffee.

Ⓑ Orange juice, chicken broth, and tea.

Ⓒ Cough syrup, hemlock, and rubbing alcohol.

⓭ When stockpiling foodstuffs for the winter, be sure to include:

Ⓐ A pound of coffee for each week, chai mix, tea, purified water, juice, rice, vegetables, fine cuts of meat, and booze.

Ⓑ 365 chicken pot pies.

Ⓒ Um...why stockpile food?

⓮ During the summer, after it's finally gotten sunny, what do you do to enjoy it?

Ⓐ Perfect your naked Slip 'n' Slide moves.

Ⓑ Wear a wide-brimmed hat and long pants when outside.

Ⓒ Check off the days until winter begins, wracked with dread.

Results

If you answered Ⓐ to most of these questions, you are a WEATHER WARRIOR. You are the Jackie Chan of overcoming the evil influence of bad weather. Your weather fighting powers border on the supernatural. We worship you. Please contact the publisher to write the second edition of *Don't Jump!*

If you answered Ⓑ to most of these questions, you are WEATHER WARY. You are simply under house arrest because of the weather. You can't go out when you want, and that ankle shackle is cramping your style. Read on!

If you answered Ⓒ to most of these questions, you are a WEATHER WIMP. You've got problems, and it's going to take the A Team to bust you out of that weather prison you're rotting in. Luckily, we are the Mr. T of weather survival. Hold tight and cover your ears, 'cuz we're going to dynamite you out of your weather funk.

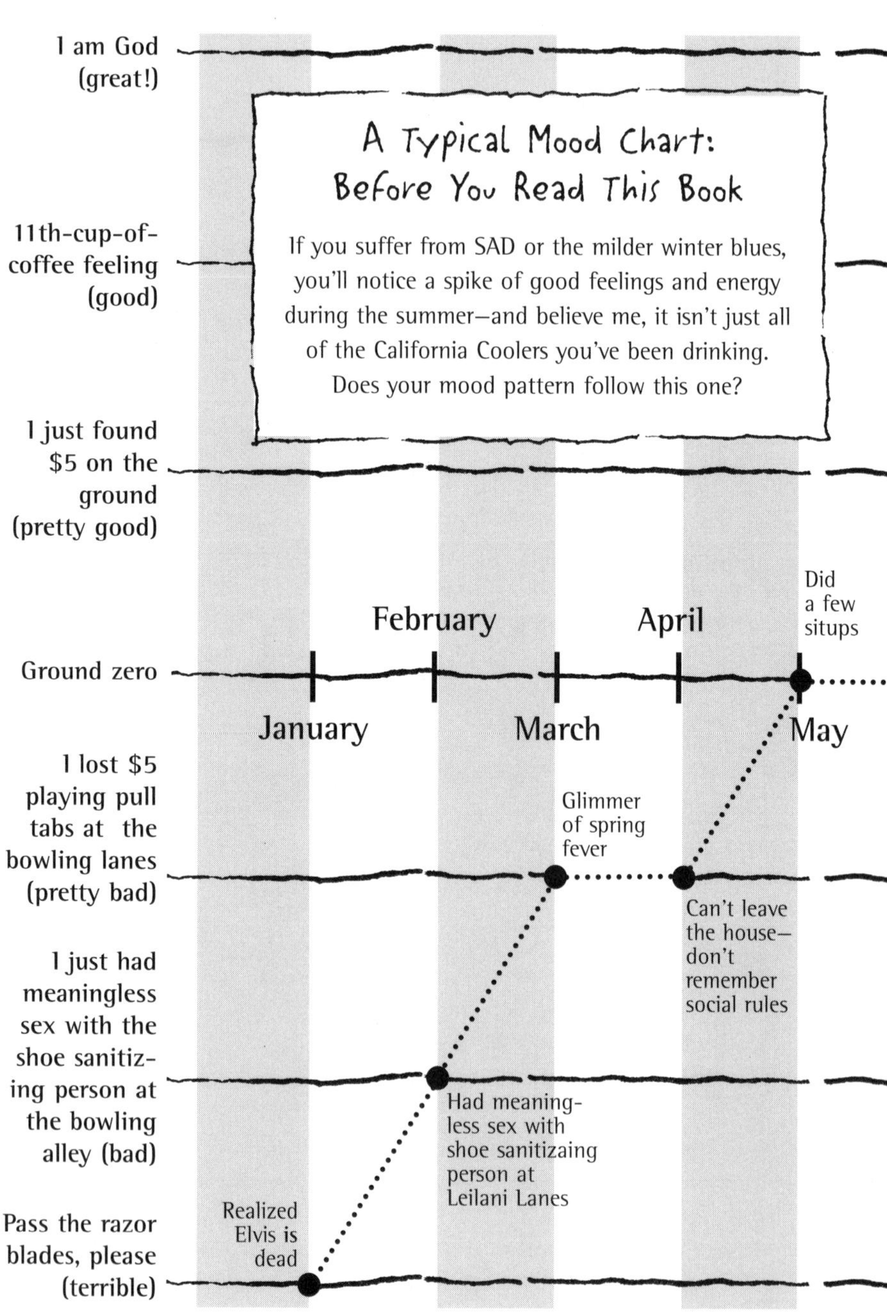
I am God (great!)
11th-cup-of-coffee feeling (good)
I just found $5 on the ground (pretty good)
Ground zero
I lost $5 playing pull tabs at the bowling lanes (pretty bad)
I just had meaningless sex with the shoe sanitizing person at the bowling alley (bad)
Pass the razor blades, please (terrible)
A Typical Mood Chart: Before You Read This Book
If you suffer from SAD or the milder winter blues, you'll notice a spike of good feelings and energy during the summer—and believe me, it isn't just all of the California Coolers you've been drinking. Does your mood pattern follow this one?
January
February
March
April
May
Realized Elvis is dead
Had meaningless sex with shoe sanitizaing person at Leilani Lanes
Glimmer of spring fever
Can't leave the house—don't remember social rules
Did a few situps

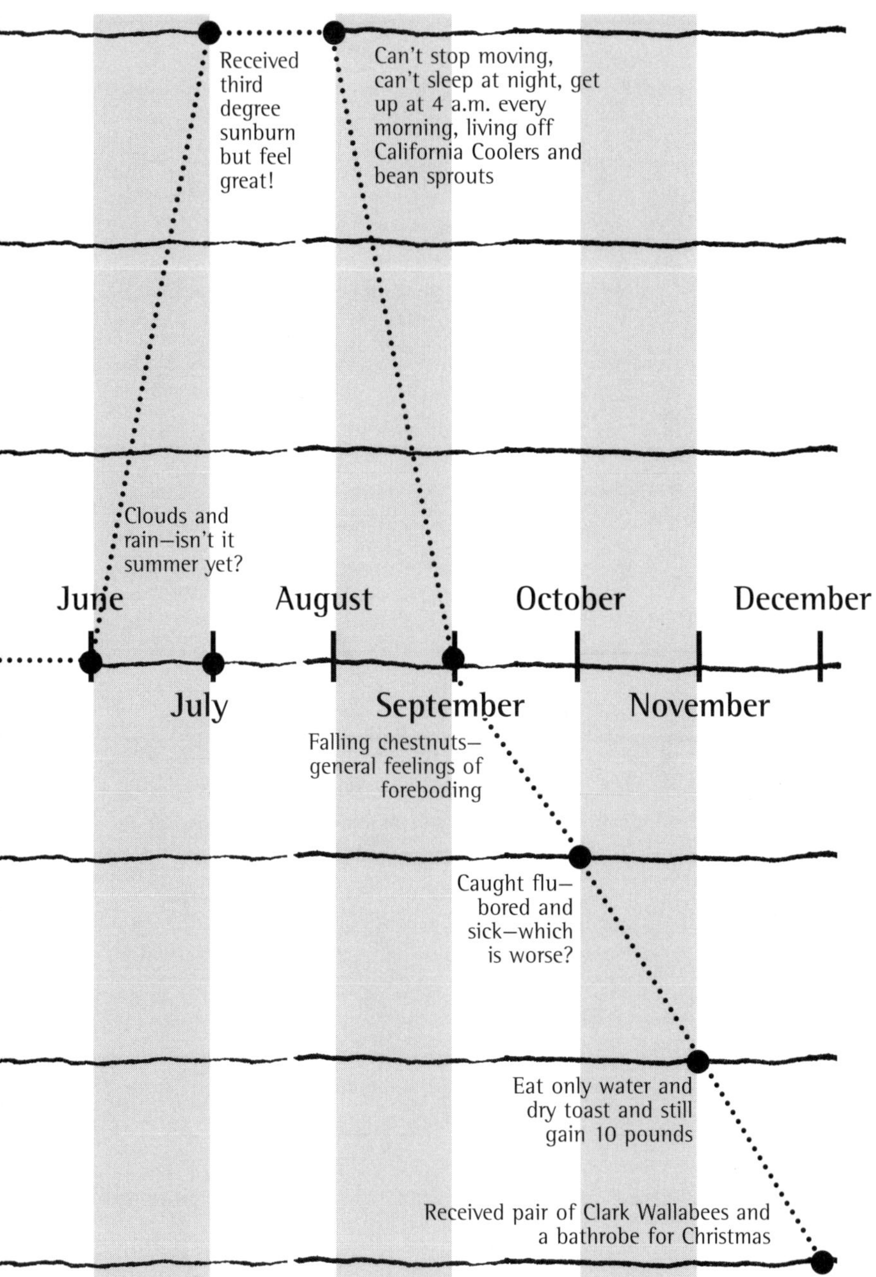
Received
third
degree
sunburn
but feel
great!
Can't stop moving,
can't sleep at night, get
up at 4 a.m. every
morning, living off
California Coolers and
bean sprouts
Clouds and
rain—isn't it
summer yet?
June
August
October
December
July
September
November
Falling chestnuts—
general feelings of
foreboding
Caught flu—
bored and
sick—which
is worse?
Eat only water and
dry toast and still
gain 10 pounds
Received pair of Clark Wallabees and
a bathrobe for Christmas

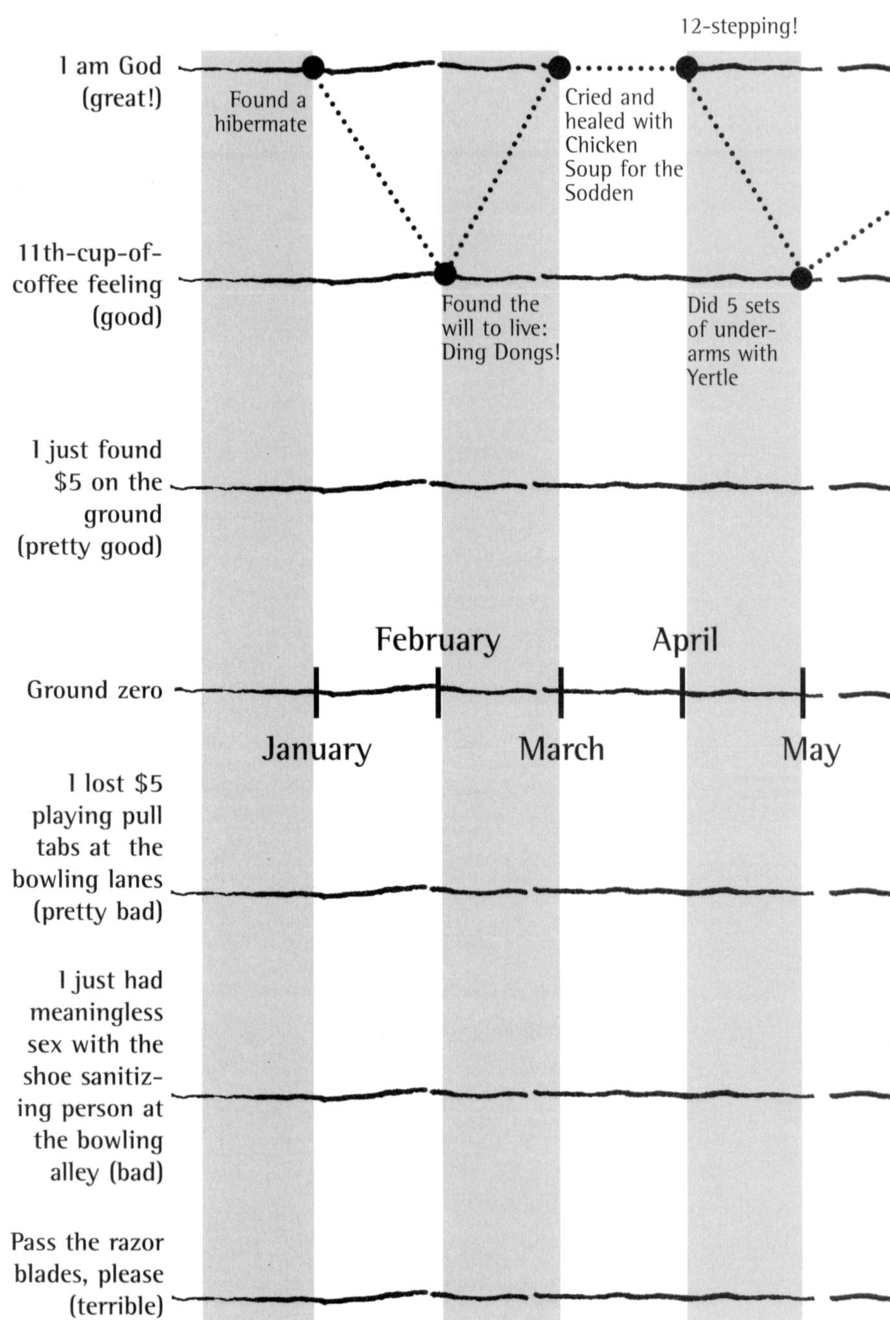
12-stepping!
I am God (great!)
Found a hibermate
Cried and healed with Chicken Soup for the Sodden
11th-cup-of-coffee feeling (good)
Found the will to live: Ding Dongs!
Did 5 sets of under-arms with Yertle
I just found $5 on the ground (pretty good)
February
April
Ground zero
January
March
May
I lost $5 playing pull tabs at the bowling lanes (pretty bad)
I just had meaningless sex with the shoe sanitizing person at the bowling alley (bad)
Pass the razor blades, please (terrible)

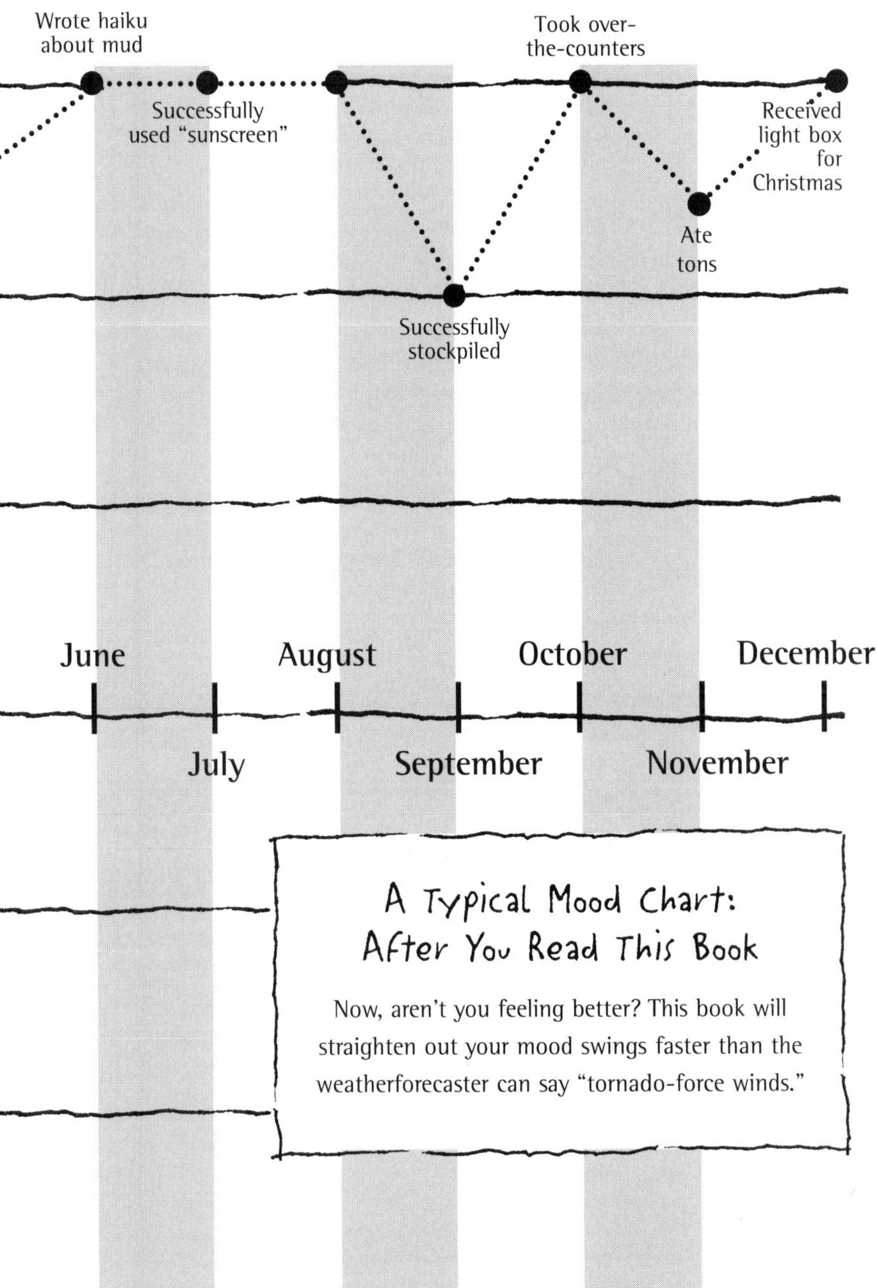

A Typical Mood Chart: After You Read This Book

Now, aren't you feeling better? This book will straighten out your mood swings faster than the weatherforecaster can say "tornado-force winds."

September: The Beginning of the End

Average Low: 52°F
Average High: 72°F
Average Rainfall: 2"

Average number of cloudy days in September: 13.2

September

September is the month of reckoning. For most of us in the Northwest, it's the last sweet gasp of summer. The month starts out warm and mild, and you run through the streets in your bikini singing "Summer Babe." But by mid-September the horse chestnut tree starts smashing spiky green nuts on your sunbathing head, and leaves that were once like fluffy green clouds drift violently across lawns, riding the howling winds of fall. The rains come and you remember, awakening from the amnesia of summer: "This is what it's like. It will be like this for eight months. I will have to turn on the heater, I will have to wear rubber products on my feet, I will overeat late into the dark evening, I will sip tea and coffee, those weak placebos for sun and light." What can you do to make yourself feel better? Make a disaster plan, silly!

Disasters That Could Occur During a Northwest Winter

Now, the impending Northwest winter isn't nearly as bad as some other disasters—like, say, the event of biological warfare or a nuclear meltdown—but it's certainly not pleasant either. Let's go through a few problems that we've encountered at the Beyond Rain and Ignorance Teaching Establishment (BRITE), and see how we battle these obstacles (see Table A).

Go ahead, make your own list! And remember, coping and surviving require an open mind and willingness to change.

Disasters	Disaster Plan
① Gain 20 pounds.	① So? It's just more cushion for the pushing.
② Get chilly in the house.	② Put a hot water bottle down the front of your pants.
③ Fade to a paler complexion.	③ Use a tanning booth and/or tanning cream; prepare to embrace the color orange.
④ Lose your sex drive.	④ Put a hot water bottle down the front of your pants.
⑤ Sleep too much.	⑤ Head to the local playground to score Ritalin from your source, "Cousin Skeeter."
⑥ Resort to wearing polar fleece.	⑥ Wear wool instead. Please. For us.
⑦ Drink heavily.	⑦ Isn't there a liquor store at Costco?
⑧ Become addicted to prescription meds/over-the-counters/marijuana.	⑧ Date a medical doctor/pharmacist/hippie.
⑨ Watch and enjoy Hogan's Heroes reruns.	⑨ This is an insurmountable obstacle. Seek psychiatric help.
⑩ Have sex with losers you pick up in singles bars.	⑩ Before going out, dab essence of cat urine on your wrists, wear a nappy gray wig, shout Tourette's syndrome–like statements, and use a walker. You'll probably still get dates (you are going to singles bars, after all), just not as many.

Table A

Survival Equipment Checklist

Speaking of survival, can we talk about stockpiling for just a second? In some ways, preparing for the Northwest autumn is like getting ready for war. You need to stock up on food, beverages, tools, and objets d'warmth for when you are trapped in your home. The quantities below are per person.

Beverages

Go ahead, ask the barista; she knows. While summer may be the time for a few dozen iced lattes, the real money starts rolling in with the rain clouds. Beginning in September, the line winds out the door, up the street, and around the corner. These people need . . . hot . . . beverages, and they need them now. This is because beverages do score (albeit low) on the Body Heat Index (see page 74).

Unfortunately, buying a beverage every day from the coffee shop adds up, and that money could go toward buying gear. Not to mention that standing in those lines exposes you to communicable diseases. To avoid such problems, you'll need to stockpile the essentials—tea, coffee, chai, hot chocolate, and booze—in your home.

- ☐ **Coffee.** One pound per week of rain. You can get this stuff everywhere. It's the drink of champions. Not only does the hot liquid warm the belly, the high caffeine content causes a feeling of well-being throughout the body. Essential.

- ☐ **Decaf Coffee.** Half-pound per month of rain. Though

many scoff at this bev, when you're trying to get through the winter but you'd like to sleep at some point, this just might work. Do not let someone you are trying to impress find out about your decaf tendencies, though, and keep your a bag of decaf beans in the far corner of your freezer, preferably disguised in a frozen fish sticks bag.

- ☐ **Chai.** Buy individually. This is the one beverage that you should have made for you, because it's complicated. The folks who swear by this stuff claim its many ingredients (cardamom, ginger, dong quai) allow the body to warm itself. We call bullshit on that: It's the caffeine in the black tea, dummy! But it still tastes good. Added bonus: The spices leave a pleasant odor on the breath—unlike coffee's dank emissions. Essential.

- ☐ **Tea.** Two pounds per month of rain. Basically, this is flavored hot water, but who's complaining? It's cheap and abundant. You'll need about two teabags per day, though come January you might be dunking up to five a day.

- ☐ **Hot Chocolate.** One 64-ounce container per month of rain. You know how they say chocolate makes you feel like you're in love? Hot chocolate makes you feel like it's sunny. Essential.

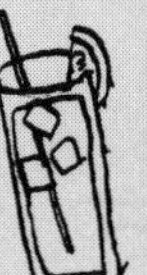

- ☐ **Booze.** Amount varies based on individual tolerance level, but estimate one bottle of your favorite hooch per week, because nothing takes the edge off a wet day like a well-poured scotch and soda—except another one in rapid succession. Right?

Food

Ahhhh, what can chase those winter blues away better than a bite of pure fat in the form of cheesecake or fudge or bacon? (Just a few necessities; your list may vary.)

- ☐ **Bacon.** One rasher per week of rain. A friend to millions. Its aroma will jolt you from even the deepest winter slumber.
- ☐ **Frozen Desserts.** One dessert per week of rain. Just one bite of a previously frozen key lime pie or a cherry cheesecake, and soon you'll be glowing like the sun (and approaching its diameter).
- ☐ **Chicken Pot Pie.** Three per week of rain. How can you resist? 100 percent of your recommended daily fat content in one small package.
- ☐ **Butter.** One pound per week of rain. Not only delicious in cookies, biscuits, and potatoes, frozen butter makes a wonderful sculpting medium. Why not carve a butter Michaelangelo, place him on a Popsicle stick, then gobble him up?

Tools

No, no, not screwdrivers and hammers. *Useful* things, like:

- ☐ Jello molds (for making jello)
- ☐ Spring-form pans (for making cheesecake)
- ☐ Juicer (fresh-squeezed orange juice tastes especially good with a splash of vodka)
- ☐ This book (distribute to friends and neighbors—if everybody isn't prepared, you'll have to share your chocolate bars)
- ☐ Breadmaker (we heart carbos)
- ☐ Blender (make frothy drinks, turn up the heater, turn on Jimmy Buffet, and have a blast with your margarita)
- ☐ Electric blanket (electromagnetic fields, schmelectromagnetic schmields)

Objets d'Warmth

Stock up on as many heat-generating bodies as you can. These may come in handy on cold winter nights.

- ☐ Pet cat (preferably declawed)
- ☐ Pet dog (Great Dane preferable to Chihuahua)
- ☐ Pet turtle (surprisingly cuddly!)
- ☐ Hot water bottle (see Disaster Plan on page 3)
- ☐ Hibermate (see the January chapter for details)

Gear Buying Guide

Chances are, you will eventually have to venture out-of-doors; be it for work or to find a hibermate, so you had better be wearing some righteous outdoor gear.

Warning: You can't buy just any type of gear. Outdoorwear is to the Northwesterner what the convertible is to the Californian: it's a serious reflection of who you actually are. Are you driving a sporty Alfa-Romeo, a sleek Mercedes, or a rusty VW Cabriolet? It all depends on where you shop.

Department Store

It is never silent in a department store. Either MTV blares away, or a piano tinkles in the background. This is because the cashiers are actually robots, and the music covers up the sound of their mechanical inner workings. There are three models of department store–clerk robots: Chipper (XR-525), Bitchy (BM-W9), and Older Lady (FUR-2000).

"Listen," we said to a Chipper, "we really want to look good, but we don't want to get all wet, either. How do we do it?" Before long, Chipper had us decked out in a pink wool poncho, embroidered jeans, dragonfly hair clips, and a pair of enormous shoes that "will lift you above the puddles." Sold.

JUST TO RECAP

What to wear to get respect: Cashmere poncho.

Attitude: My platinum card just got approved.

Never: Spill your beverage on an employee; you will be electrocuted.

Tip: DKNY is not pronounced "Dinky."

What to buy: Dragonfly hair clips, $15; beaded cashmere scarf, $68; leopard-skin fuzzy slippers, $40.

Outdoor Store

Going to an outdoor store to buy gear is a religious experience for some Northwest residents. The stores—expansive, airy—are similar to places of worship and, as in synagogues, cathedrals, and mosques, there are rules you must abide by.

Rule ① Never speak to the employees until they speak to you first. The Employee is equivalent to a priest/rabbi/holy man, and has earned his/her position by forsaking television and potato chips, existing on a diet of PowerBars, and repeatedly proving him/herself on the climbing wall.

Rule ② Dress appropriately. Traditional garb includes polar fleece, thermal underwear, micro-fleece beany on head, Gore-Tex boots. If you are not dressed as such, the Employee will not speak to you.

Rule ③ The display sections represent religious iconography, similar to the stations of the cross in a Catholic church. Never giggle or point at these scenes of camping, climbing, or skiing bliss.

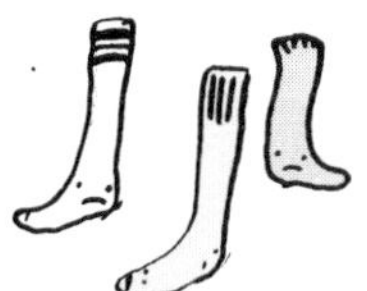

JUST TO RECAP

What to wear to get respect: Traditional outdoor gear; borrow if need be.

Attitude: Holy reverence.

Never: Stop to rest on the rocks strewn about the store. Not only does this make you look lazy, they're fake and could crumble under your bulk.

Tip: When speaking to the Employee, mention your subscription to *Outside* magazine (a bit like reciting passages from the Torah to a rabbi).
What to buy: Gore-Tex shell, $350; Gore-Tex boots, $350; special baseline mid-layer underwear, $25 per piece.

Army/Navy Surplus Store

The first thing you notice when you walk through the doors of an Army/Navy surplus store is all the stuff you don't and will never need (but might want). Things like military pins and combat helmets, grenades and gas masks, videos called *Police Officer Restraining Techniques*—that sort of thing. But this type of store contains tons of things that you do need, so pay attention. Ask yourself: Am I ready, really ready? Do a couple of deep knee bends. Then march up to Buzz or Rudy or whatever his name is behind the knife display and demand his opinion about what to buy for the impending winter. Boonie cap? MP3 arctic parka with fur-lined hood? Minus-10-degree boots? Then prepare yourself to be disappointed, as we were.

"Honey, what's your name?" Buzz asked and patted our shoulder. "Now calm down. Breathe.

"These boonie caps are made exclusively for jungle warfare. The rain actually goes through these so they don't rot in jungles. Why don't you just get a wool cap? Come with me to the dressing room, we'll get you all straightened out!"

Before you know it, Buzz is handing you urban camouflage, flannel shirts, and cargo pants, and clicking his tongue, "Girl, you look good!"

What, no arctic parachute pants? No snow parkas? No. "Maybe get some thermal underwear, some wool socks." The craziest things Buzz recommended were some waterproof Sorel boots.

JUST TO RECAP (YAWN . . .)

What to wear to get respect: Urban camouflage.

Attitude: I'm not crazy, I'm not crazy.

Never: Pull the pin out of the grenade. Very uncool.

Tip: Turns out Army/Navy surplus stores are headquarters for fashion in the Northwest.

What to buy: Wool socks, $15 per pair; thermal underwear, $10 per piece; Sorel boots, $135.

Rough Winter Ahead? Signs from the Natural World

Farmers and sages have guessed at the character of the upcoming winter using clues from the natural world: The width of the woolly bear caterpillar's stripe, a careful dissection of a pig's spleen, or the number of nuts squirrels gather in the fall all were indicators of the severity of the upcoming winter. Nowadays, people tend to pooh-pooh these methods, but at BRITE, we firmly believe cues taken from the natural world can predict changes in the weather. From years of observation, we've culled four of the most accurate signs.

1. The Whipped Cream Gauge

Go into a coffee shop in September. Order a hot chocolate or mocha with whipped cream. Measure the centimeters of whipped cream that extend above the edge of the cup.

- If there is 1 or fewer centimeters, expect a mild winter.

- If there are 2 to 3 centimeters, expect a harsh winter with lots of snow.
- If there are more than 3 centimeters of whip, expect a winter full of blizzards, ice storms, and gale-force winds. Tip your barista excessively.

2. Rings on Hippies

Go to a place that hippies frequent (dog parks, drum circles, hemp stores) and observe the jewelry they are wearing.

- If they are wearing turquoise rings on all of their fingers, the winter will be especially harsh with lots of snowfall.
- If they wear a few simple silver rings, the winter will be very dry but cold.
- If they are wearing long dangling earrings, expect strong winds and ice storms.
- If they are wearing toe rings, expect a mild but rainy winter with some flooding.

3. Karaoke Predictions

Go to your favorite karaoke bar. Jot down the songs performed.

- If anything by Prince is sung, the winter will be wet and moody.
- A performance of Eddie Grant's "Electric Avenue" means only one thing: a mild, dry winter, with some warm winds blowing in from the south.
- If someone performs Olivia Newton John's "Physical," expect a windy winter; add torrential rains if a duet from *Grease* follows.
- A performance of "I Will Survive" means a wet winter without snow.

4. Counting Crazies

Late at night, board a bus. Make note of the type and number of insane passengers.*

- If you notice more mutterers than sleepers, it'll be a mild winter.
- If you encounter someone shouting about Satan, Jesus, Buddha, or any other popular religious figure, plan on a wet winter with some thunderstorms.
- If someone sings a song in the voice of Phyllis Diller from the back of the bus, the winter will be snowy, long, and excruciatingly painful.

*Special bonus predictor: Count the number of greasy head spots on the bus windows; if there are more than three, expect lots of foggy mornings.

Northwest Weather Persona

Grizzled Adams

Umbrella: Hell, no.

Winter gripe: Animals are all hibernating.

Coping mechanism: Four-wheel-driving in mud.

If anyone's ready for the weather, this guy is. He's been stockpiling for years at the Army/Navy surplus store, not to mention the three elk in his freezer. His big truck makes it through even the biggest puddles. Yeeee-haaawwww!

October: Don't Touch Me, I'm Sick

Average Low: 45°F
Average High: 62°F
Average Rainfall: 3"

The average adult catches four to six colds per year.

October

Look, let's face it, it's October and soon you will fall ill. Maybe a slight cold with a runny nose, or maybe full-blown pneumonia. Why do we get sick more often during the winter than in the summer? Perhaps the crowded, moist buses and buildings we frequent are breeding grounds for germs. Maybe your body has to work harder to stay warm because of the

The Many Meanings of "Bless You" . . . Including "You're About to Die!"

You've just released 100-mile-per-hour winds out your mouth and nose, blowing snot all over the person sitting on the bus in front of you. Everyone has a blessing for you. What does each of these sayings really mean?

Bless you: You are getting sick and you might die.

God bless you: Your soul just left the bus, and I think I saw a demon sneak in.

"You little shit!": You just blew snot on my neck.

"Gesundheit": *Health* in German.

"Health!": I'm a German tourist.

"Shut up!": I'm a tourist from New York.

"Can't you hold those?": I'm a hypochondriac.

Silence: We all hate you.

cold weather, thus running down your immune system. Or could it be that the unrelenting rain has demented your brain, and you are under the control of voices in your head that order you to lick public telephones and bus handrails?

Just the FAQs

Here's a list of the most frequently asked questions about colds and flus that we receive at BRITE.

Q: What's the difference between a cold and a flu?

A: When you have a cold, your friends will ask how you're feeling. When you have the flu, they'll ask if you've ever thought about wearing a surgical mask.

Q: If I catch the flu, what will it be like?

A: What? Are you an idiot? It'll be hell. Your nose will produce alarming amounts of fluid, loved ones will flee from you, you'll sit in bed for days, you'll sleep all day, you'll have a fever, a hacking cough, and throat soreness. On the positive side, you can call in sick to work, and someone might send you flowers.

Q: What's sinusitis?

A: Your sinuses are cavities behind your nose—we're not sure how they got there, but if "secretions" build up and bacteria get in them, you've got sinusitis, which usually results in an extremely painful headache. The upside? Painkillers! Ferret away some of these for a money-making venture after you've recovered.

Q: How do I know if I have a chest infection?

A: It'll itch like hell . . . oh, a *chest* infection; hmmm, we dunno . . . .

Q: Is it polite to blow your nose at the dinner table?

A: Yes, but don't use the tablecloth.

Q: I just got over a cold, and two days later I'm sick again. What gives?

A: Tragically, you've developed a new type of cold. This sort of bad luck is like being diagnosed with cancer and then having a stroke; or like washing your car, only to have it run over by a cement truck. Call it God's will or move to a different state because, baby, you're cursed.

Prevention

After reading about the terrible things a cold or flu will do to you, you must be shaking in your boots. Cold prevention is not an exact science—it falls somewhere between hypnotizing chickens and bloodletting. But everyone has a couple of gem suggestions.

Pragmatic Suggestions from Mom

- Stop touching those dirty handrails on the bus!
- Put this scarf that I knitted around your neck if your throat starts to hurt—your skin looks wonderful against baby-poop orange.
- Wash your hands after playing with children—when are you going to have children?
- Get a flu shot—I'll send you a check to help pay for it, I know you're struggling financially.
- Take those vitamin C and multivitamin pills I sent you last Christmas.

Preventive Methods of the Anally Retentive

Not worried about what others think? Prepared to go that extra mile to avoid illness?

- ☐ Wear a surgical mask at all times. Your only consolation is that Michael Jackson used to wear one. Didn't he?
- ☐ Disinfect all utensils in your home, including hairbrush, toothbrush, fork, and spoon.
- ☐ Wear latex gloves. Some might find this sexy. Don them every time you might come in contact with something someone else has touched, and you don't have time to disinfect the item. Wear them before using public phones, shaking hands, and shopping in stores.
- ☐ Sleep in a bubble.

The Way of the Healthy Hippie

Ever wondered why you've never seen a sick hippie? They're always smiling and dancing that hippie dance. They have many secrets for cold and flu prevention!

- Zinc is apparently an anti-oxidant that protects against free radical damage to cells. Helps to "smoke a bowl" while the zinc lozenge dissolves under your tongue. Tastes gross.
- These dreadlocked children of the earth are suckers for L-O-V-E, and believe it boosts the immune system. If you're a nonbeliever, just try saying a few of these statements for a week: "It's all good." "Mellow greetings." "Go where the flow takes you." Who knows? Maybe you'll give away all your earthly possessions and start living in a van, in addition to feeling healthy.
- Chinese herbs like Yin Chao are often used by hippies to prevent colds. These tiny green pills are supposed to stop a cold if taken in the early stages. You have to choke down five to eight pills at once, but they make a nice clicking noise going down your throat.
- Echinacea tincture is made from a pretty flower's roots steeped in vodka. Tastes like a stewed Birkenstock, but the alcohol makes it worthwhile. Hey, that's why hippies are so happy!

Hairdo Options for Maximum Warmth

The Farrah Fawcett (aka helmet hair)
All that hair spray and curl make the wearer's head impermeable to cold drafts.

The Mullet
The long hair in the back creates a scarf of warmth on the wearer's neck. Mullets with a perm in back are frequently spotted at soccer matches. Warning: Keep a safe distance behind a wet mullet. One head-toss and you're soaked.

Dreadlocks
Stupid if you aren't a Rastafarian, but grease in hair does repel rain incredibly well.

Full Beard
Simple fact: Hair retains heat.

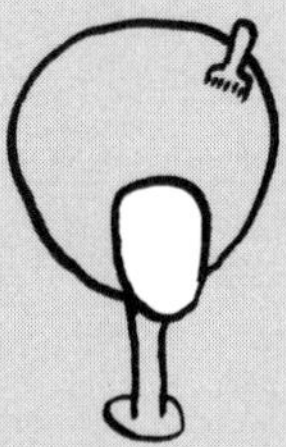

The Afro
A halo of warmth. Comb optional.

Hairdo Options for Minimum Warmth

Bald
Brrr! If you can avoid this condition, do.

The Mohawk
Looks cool, but that strip of hair does nothing for you.

Mustache
A 'stash immediately decreases your chance of finding a hibermate, but your upper lip sure will be cozy.

Pigtails
Very cute, but reduces hat-wearing capabilities.

When You Do Get Sick: Drug Talk

Even if you live in a bubble, you'll catch something. But, hey, being sick isn't all that bad. It's a time to experiment with many kinds of drugs, to sleep a lot, to feel bored—sorta like college. Who says over-the-counters can't be gateway drugs?

Decongestant

Purpose: Unclogs stuffy sinuses.
Side effects: Sleepiness.
Overdose fun: If you take, say, nine tablets instead of the recommended two, you'll be able to read and write Sanskrit without any prior knowledge.

Cough Syrup

Purpose: Knocks you out so you won't cough.
Side effects: Sleepiness.
Overdose fun: If the syrup contains codeine and you double the recommended dosage, be prepared to levitate your entire body, and then puke into the toilet bowl for three hours straight.

Ibuprofen

Purpose: Takes away fever, muscle aches, headaches.
Side effects: Heartburn.
Overdose fun: Take too many of these, and you'll be doing a stomach-lining striptease.

Expectorant

Purpose: Loosens mucus so you can cough it up.
Side effects: Repulsive hacking noises and loogies.
Overdose fun: Dazzle people by coughing up your stomach!

To Have a Flu Shot or Not?

You should. It isn't expensive (usually $10–$20 at a clinic), and it usually works to prevent the season's flu. The real trouble begins with the people you will meet when you go to get the shot.

Shot givers: Hey, wasn't this guying selling newspapers at the grocery store last week?

Sickies: These people develop a full-blown flu within five minutes of getting the shot.

Gawkers: The clinic might attract people who aren't getting a shot but who insist on watching everyone else and providing running commentary. "Hey! He just fainted, what a wimp!"

Hypochondriacs: Will ask shot giver to sterilize their entire arm before the injection. Identified by body bubble.

Fainters: Some people don't know they are afraid of needles until they get to the clinic. They will faint once they get the shot. Steal their cookies.

Things to Do in Bed

One of the worst symptoms of a cold or flu is boredom. And they don't sell a cure for that at the grocery store. Well, you're right, they do sell 40-ouncers there, but that's not recommended when you're ill. BRITE has developed and tested several activities to while away the days in bed when you have nothing to do but sleep and blow your nose.

Supermodel Fun

Cut out magazine photos of supermodels. Remove their heads using (1) a knife, (2) your teeth, (3) BB-gun bullets fired from across the room. Reserve a few with heads, and hang them by dental-floss nooses near your bed. Don't you feel better already? If people come to visit, hide them.

Tissue Sculpture

All you need is snot and toilet paper, and when you're sick you'll have plenty of both. Snot is an amazing adhesive. Start by making something simple, like a snowman. Glom three sheets of tissue together for the base, two for the snowman's thorax, and one crumpled tissue for the head. Decorate with things from the side of the bed: toothpick arms, dental-floss scarf, two dried boogers for eyes. As you develop your skill, try making more-complicated forms like dogs, Ferris wheels, and cars with vitamin C wheels; give them to small children once you recover.

Fever Babbling

When one is in the throes of a 102-degree fever, hallucinations occur. Capitalize on your dementia by tape-recording yourself describing what you see. Once the fever breaks, listen to these ramblings and paint what you described. Step aside, Dali!

Cat Beauty School

Kitty's just as bored as you—why not give her a new hairdo? The cat mohawk is simple: Apply hair-removal solution to the cat's entire body except for a thin strip along the backbone, wrap the cat in a towel for 10 minutes, then wash off. If you have lots of time, paint its claws and dye its fur pink while you're at it. Every time you see kitty, it'll be a reminder of your creativity.

Stomach Reggae

Since you've been ingesting so much orange juice, chicken soup, and water, why not learn to use your sloshing belly as a musical instrument? Play along with relatively simple music, like reggae, by slapping, shaking, and shimmying your stomach to the beat. Smoking a bit of reefer really adds another dimension, but may make you feel as if you have more talent than you actually do.

Vitamin C Beadwork

This craft staves off boredom and can generate some money. Tools: varying sizes of vitamin C, hemp twine, necklace clip. Drill holes in the vitamins with any sharp object. Begin stringing the twine through them. With each addition to the growing string, make a knot to secure the vitamin. Add clips at the ends for fastening. For variety, you may use other types of pills, including aspirin and cough drops. (Caution: Do not use gel caps.) After you've recovered, try selling these on a little blanket downtown.

Ventriloquist Fun

Lonely in bed? How about creating a hot-water-bottle sidekick! Think up a personality first—childish? aristocratic? goofy?—then glue some hair and paint a face onto your hot water bottle. Entertain friends by holding your new rubber buddy up to your face while you talk—give him or her a cute lisp or another endearing speech impediment. Vegas, here we come!

Northwest Weather Persona

Web Fortran

Umbrella: Not necessary; he doesn't go outside.

Winter gripe: Loud rain makes noise on the roof—breaking his concentration on programming.

Coping mechanism: Sunshine screen saver.

Little Webbie can't get enough of his computer, no matter what the season. Unless there's a big enough storm to knock the power out, he couldn't care less.

November: Must . . . Eat . . . More

Average Low: 40°F
Average High: 52°F
Average Rainfall: 6"

Average weight gained by Americans during winter: 10-20 lbs.

Dear Diary:
I found my first stretch mark of the season. Upper-right side. Hip region. I wept big, cholesterol-packed tears onto my candy bar.

If this diary entry sounds familiar, you may be possessed by the winter soul. And we're not talking about Santa Claus and good cheer and eggnog . . . well, maybe the eggnog . . . but, the point is, as you get closer and closer to winter, you'll notice that an entity possesses the body and convinces you to partake in excessive activities, including overeating, oversleeping, and binge drinking. This is the force of the winter soul. Think back to summer when you used to nibble on a bean sprout and then put it down (half eaten) and run outside for more Slip 'n' Slide fun. It's not like that anymore. No, no, things are very different.

Listening to Food

Go to the supermarket in November and have a look around if you don't believe us. What do you see? Food, right? But look closer and tune in, because all of that food is trying to communicate with you and your winter soul. Following is a tour of what the supermarket kingdom might say:

Vegetable Aisle

Potatoes: Pick up this little spud and put it next to your ear. Like the masochistic little tuber it is, it calls out, "Mash me, mash me. Drizzle my mashed innards with butter. Pour hot animal fats over my creamy, tender flesh. Bake me at 350 degrees for one hour, then slice me open and slather me with sour cream, butter, and three kinds of cheese." We're not making this up—we've heard russets, yellow Finns, and red and purple potatoes beg like this.

Lettuce, bean sprouts, anything more than 80 percent water: "Dear John: You know, I really like you and we've had lots of good times together, but frankly, when you use that salad spinner, it makes me feel cheap." Put down that drippy rabbit food immediately!

Tomato: "Ahhhh, yeah. Hi. Um. Hi. I've been living in a warehouse, down by the river for oh"—deep breath—"about 14 months now. I haven't really had a lot of time to socialize. I feel like my insides are mealy. Are you still there? Oh, good. You know, I liked it there in the dark, but I don't know, when I got out, I was red on the outside, but on the inside, man, I'm still green. You know? Hello? Hello?"

Meat Aisle

Pork products, including that devil bacon: After a pig becomes meat, it's unstoppably charming! "Darling. You look fab. Kiss, kiss. Are those new shoes? And a matching handbag? Yummy! Listen, doll, can you get me out of this dump? I mean, look who I'm surrounded by—what is this, some low-budget production of *Animal Farm?*" How can you resist?!

Beef, another charmer: "No, I want to know how *you* are. Are they still working you to death at that job? You deserve better! And your dear mother, how is she? Oh, you're mad at her; well, she *can* be trying, can't she? Tell me all about it; let's go get a pedicure."

Please pause for a moment or two here. Take a few deep breaths if need be, but don't look like a freak and stare at your fellow customers. Just pretend that you are making a shopping list. Or are really grooving to the Muzak. We want to tell you not to worry—you aren't crazy! Everyone hears the food talking to them; look at those full carts just brimming with fattening foodstuffs! It's the ghoulish power of your winter soul! Now, make a few self-affirmations like "I'm cute" or "I'd marry me" before we move on to the . . .

Bakery Department

As you walk toward the bakery section, you'll hear a steady murmur that eventually becomes a roar! The voices are just bouncing off the glass cases and into your ear hole. You can't make out any distinct voices, just a steady chant:

"Hey-hey, hey-ho, these pastry products have got to go. What do we want? Someone to stuff us into their mouth. When do we want it? Now!" Run with these socially just, union-member doughnuts under your arm.

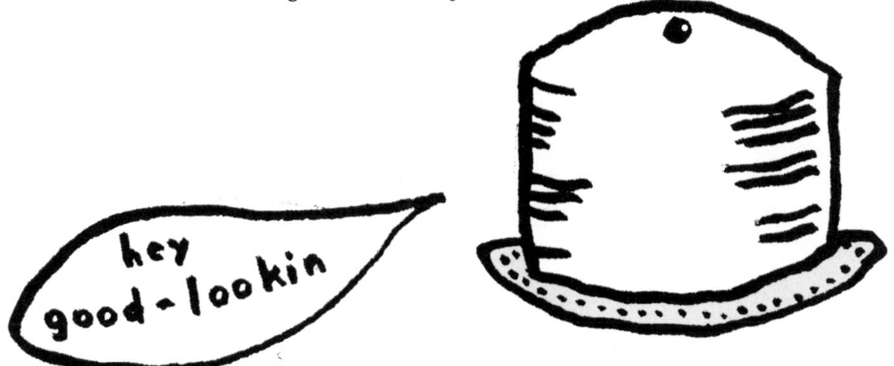

Freezer Section

As in a 19th-century Russian novel, there is a cacophony of voices coming from deep within your store's ice chests. Most of them are moaning about being cold, so cold. Especially sad are the Sara Lee Thaw and Serve cheesecakes. A Southerner does not last long in the freezer section! Only you can save her!

Also, that vixen Marie Callender is whispering sweet nothings into your ear: "Real chunks of chicken. Flaky butter crust." Just don't look at her nutritional chart because one M.C. pie contains 200 percent of your recommended daily fat allowance! "Don't look, love; believe me, we don't need to think about that, now, do we?" She's got a point . . .

Now that you've heard the voices of the supermarket wooing your winter soul, start listening to the food items in your house—that Halloween candy that's still hanging around, Thanksgiving leftovers . . . and, face it, you're beat.

If You Can't Beat 'Em, Join 'Em: How to Find an Eating Partner

Remember how the Indians saved the pilgrims from starving that autumn long ago? That was nice! Following in that giving tradition, we aren't going to recommend depriving yourself this winter. Here's our suggested diet plan: Find an eating partner, eat tons, and blame the cleaned plates on each other. Obviously, find a partner who likes the kinds of food you enjoy eating too much of. The only way to ensure food compatibility is to go directly to the sumptuous source.

Barbecue Buddy

Linger at a roadside barbecue stand. Watch what each customer orders. Choose the person loading up on the most pulled-pork sandwiches. Soon you'll be smearing each other's bodies with barbecue sauce.

Pick-up line: "Can I lick your fingers?"

Doughnut Doppelganger

Travel to the doughnut shop at night. The real doughnut aficionados eat these sweet treats before they go to bed, not in the morning like everybody else. Anybody ordering a wide selection of jellies, chocolate-covered, and old-fashions is a prime contender for a beautiful eating friendship.

Tip: Be sure to put a touch of doughnut cologne on your wrists to get that special someone's attention.

Pick-up line: "Can I help you dunk that?"

Beef Jerky Jim-dandy

Go to the beef jerky outlet store. Scoop up the babe buying the bag of beef jerky odds and ends.

Tip: Never ask these folks if they know where beef jerky comes from.

Pick-up line: "Can you help me find the jerky chew aisle?"

Dim Sum Delight

Begin dining on a Sunday at 10 a.m. Through the mist and clanging carts, look for someone eating alone. Count his or her plates. If your prospective eating partner is still racking up the dishes at 3 p.m., consider approaching him or her.

Pick-up tactic: Slip your phone number in the lucky diner's fortune cookie.

Fried-chicken Chum

Nothing like a restaurant filled with chicken grease to help find an eating partner. Zero in on the guy or gal buying extra biscuits with plenty of bird.

Pick-up line: "Can I eat your giblets?"

Freezer-case Friends

Hang out in the freezer section of the grocery store. (Bundle up before you go!) Approach anyone seen buying more than five chicken pot pies or a cartful of ice cream.

Pick-up line: "Do you need help melting those?" Then lick finger and press to your bottom while making a sizzling noise. Wink.

Now that you know how to find an eating partner, why not have a different one for each of your favorite kinds of food? Get out there and go hog-wild!

Chapped Lips: Why in the Winter?

As all that food passes across your lips, you might notice your lips are getting chapped. BRITE has found a higher incidence of chapped lips during the cold months. We believe dry, chapped lips are caused by fall and winter's winds and from dry indoor air, all of which rob your lips of moisture. Since eating barbecue becomes painful with cracked lips, you'd better figure out the best way of taking care of this problem.

Here are a few suggested remedies that also might bring your eating partner's lips closer to yours:

- ☐ **Emu oil.** Go to enough farmers markets or malls and you'll eventually find someone hawking this stuff along with some really large black eggs. The oil comes from the ugly emu (which have never had chapped lips a day in their lives).
- ☐ **Carmex.** Comes in a strange yellow container and smells like a doctor's office. Some people swear by it.
- ☐ **Bag Balm.** The farmer's secret weapon against sore teats and udders works on your lips too. Slather some on and make your favorite barnyard animal sounds.
- ☐ **Flavored lip balms.** Who can resist flavors like grape, Dr. Pepper, and chocolate on your lips? And dieters: Why not just eat these?
- ☐ **Lip gloss.** So '80s and so so sexy! You won't even be able to feel your lips beneath a couple coats of this stuff.
- ☐ **Butter.** Not just for cookies anymore, your friend butter will protect your lips against the harshest storms. Just carry a stick in your purse.
- ☐ **Chicken grease.** After spending an entire week eating only chicken, some of the BRITE scientists noticed their lips weren't chapped anymore. Coincidence? We think not.

A Moderne Foodal: Symbolic Meanings of Junk Food

In medieval times, each herb and plant symbolized a different feeling or attribute. Symbolic plants were given as disguised messages; for instance, Ophelia gave Hamlet rosemary for remembrance before she jumped into the river. These days, though, no one remembers these old symbols, so in a nod to modern times, we've created a new palette of symbolism based on—yes—snack foods. Keep these in mind when sending or receiving gifts of foodstuffs.

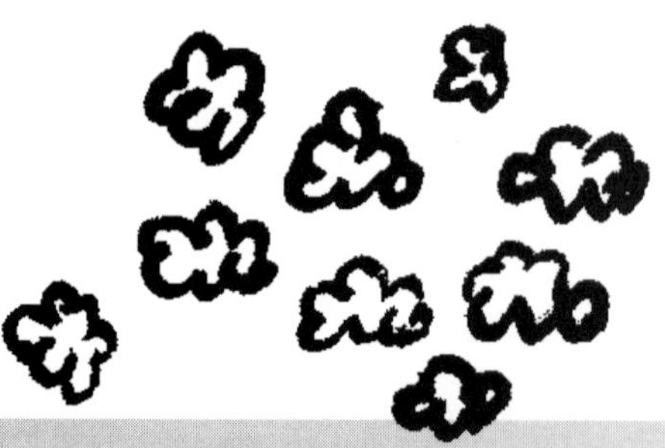

Junk Food	Meaning
Animal crackers	Sacrifice
Beef jerky	Courage, strength
Chocolate wafers	PMS
Doughnuts	Law and Order
French fries	Glory
Fruit Roll-Ups	Yoga
Graham crackers	Youth
Gummi bears or fish	Big eyes
Licorice, black	Maturity
Licorice, red	Eternal love
Onion rings	Forbearance
Peanuts	Patriotism
Pepperoni sticks	Flatulence
Pistachios	Envy
Popcorn, plain	Anxiety
Popcorn, cheese	Friendship
Popcorn, caramel	Patience
Pork rinds	Sympathy
Pretzels	Confusion
Mints	Eternal refreshment
Shrimp chips	Bad breath
Tortilla chips	Comfort

Ways to Disguise Your Winter Body

It is of the utmost importance that you put food in your mouth to avoid boredom and to raise your spirits during the winter doldrums, and it's well known that you *need* that layer of fat to survive the cold winter. However, there is the chance that you might not want your new winter fat to draw attention to itself, like an obnoxious relative. Here are some tips.

① **Flashy shoes.** Blissfully, your feet don't gain much weight, no matter how much butter you eat. Buy some loud shoes—think lime green jogging shoes, beaded cowboy boots, or fringed platform sandals—people will stare at them instead of your belly.

② **Skater clothes.** The kids are wearing the baggiest gear these days; why not take advantage of this fat-hiding apparel? Your new baggy pants and shirts might be misconstrued as signs of a midlife crisis but, what the heck, that'll throw them off your flabby trail.

③ **Never wear floral blouses.** They scream "maternity wear." Ask yourself: Are you mentally prepared for someone to ask you if you're pregnant?

④ **Tanning booths.** Universal truth: Orange looks thinner than white.

November Diary

Refer back to these notes next year, so you will be better prepared.

Foods that communicated with me via my winter soul:

___

___

___

Methods used to convince me to eat the particular food item:

___

___

___

Did I find an eating partner in November?

___

If yes, where did I find him/her? What food craving did we both share?

___

___

___

If no, what's wrong with me?

___

___

___

___

What methods did I utilize to hide my newly acquired bulk?

___

___

Northwest Weather Persona

Ima Toorich

Umbrella: Yes; the largest money can buy.

Winter gripe: Must run to SUV to avoid the rain.

Coping mechanism: Prada.

Bad weather affects the rich, too, but barely. They don't have to worry about wet socks (just throw them away), weight gain (personal trainer), or not enough light (vacations to Bermuda).

December: Down and Out

Average Low: 36°F
Average High: 46°F
Average Rainfall: 6"

Average number of daylight hours in the Northwest during December: 9

December

Darkness has fallen, my sweet. December is the month for depression. Why? Because you're supposed to spend time with people to whom you wish you weren't related, buy overpriced gifts, receive hideous presents with grace—all of this with only a few hours of precious daylight. The only way for many people to make it through this month is to imagine that an overweight man dressed in red velvet will sneak into their home and improve their material well-being. If that's the best we can come up with, everyone should be jumping off the bridge. But don't do it! No, really. Now, come on, move away from the edge. We mean it. Here's a chocolate bar. OK, good.

All I Want for Christmas Is My Two Front Teeth . . . Wait a Minute, Screw That!

In the northern latitudes, holidays featuring light are traditionally celebrated during the dark, bleak month of December, and with celebration comes gift giving. It goes without saying that if you embrace more religions, you can score more presents. Who said holidays aren't about stockpiling? So let's get that wish list started!

- ☐ **All I want for Hanukkah (eight days = more gifts!) is:** A goose-down comforter; light box; silk long underwear; tanning booth time; featherbed; full-spectrum lightbulbs; two bottles of whiskey; flannel sheets.
- ☐ **All I want for Christmas is:** A 4x4 vehicle with an air-brushed Jesus Christ on the hood.
- ☐ **All I want for Kwanzaa is:** A plane ticket to Hawaii.
- ☐ **All I want for Winter Solstice is:** An oak-embossed standing altar and thousands of aromatherapy candles.
- ☐ **All I want for Lord Parshvanath's birth is:** A computer with a T-1 connection and a bevy of software.
- ☐ **All I want for Fête des Membres is:** Nintendo Game Boy.

Got Depression? Some Cures for the Winter Blues

At the BRITE laboratories, we're constantly testing innovative treatments for the winter blues (for more hard-core remedies, see February's "Guide to Antidepressants" Guide. Here are some of our latest discoveries:

Light Box (ask physician before buying)

Cost: $150–$450.
Available: At the Indoor Sun Shoppe (911 NE 45th, Seattle); from The SunBox Company (19217 Orbit Drive, Gaithersburg, MD 20879); at various Group Health Take Care Stores; at Zenith Supplies (6300 Roosevelt Way, Seattle); or on-line at www.nu-light.com, www.bio-light.com, and www.hlt.com.

Though light boxes look plain, they pack a punch. Folks who sit in front of them for a couple hours a day report feeling a lessening of the effects of winter depression. These clunky refrigerator door–looking things will replace your best friend. And at prices like these, they should.

Dawn Simulator

Cost: $149.
Available: Through Outside/In at www.bodyclock.com/nac2.htm or www.healthyenvironments.com/.

No, not *stimulator*, you dirty bird! This device *simulates* dawn by slowly adding light to your bedroom on those dark winter mornings. We like the rounded ones from Outside/In. They look super-space age. This little gem isn't totally essential for people with winter depression, but it helps with getting people up on time for work, and generally makes mornings bearable.

Light Visor

Cost: $299.
Available: At www.lighttherapyproducts.com.

Much like those collars you put on dogs so they won't gnaw on their wounds, this device may seem like it was made to humiliate you. Not even the beautiful model in the brochure looks good with this on. But the visor is in fact good for you. It's like a portable light box that you can wear while exercising. But don't be surprised if people gawk and point while you jog around the neighborhood.

Chinese Medicine

Cost: $10–$100.
Available: At Chinese pharmacies and naturopath(et)ic medicine clinics like Bastyr.

According to Chinese medicine, yin equals dark, cold, and wet, while yang means light, hot, and dry. During the winter, your yin might overpower your yang and upset the body's quest for balance. Winter is also prime time for the emotion of fear because it is a season that reminds us of death—dead trees, darkness, and visits to your grandmother's house.

Methods like acupuncture (needles), moxibustion (burning leaves), and cupping (hot suction cups), in addition to taking Chinese herbs, might alleviate your winter depression. Most of the tinctures and teas taste very, very bad. We've found that Chinese food—especially items like Kung Pao chicken, won-ton soups, and Shanghai noodles—can also be quite effective in reducing winter blues.

Natural Remedies: Vitamin D and St. John's Wort

Cost: $10.
Available: At health food stores and on-line at www.mothernature.com.

The majority of vitamin D in the body is created during a chemical reaction that starts with sunlight exposure to the skin, so it follows that your body may have a lack of vitamin D during the winter, thus making you depressed.

Even though the word "wort" is unattractive, St. John's wort has been shown to alleviate symptoms of depression. Warning: Another popular anti-depressant, beer, has been known to taste "weird" when taken in conjunction with St. John's wort. For God's sake, be careful!

Exercise: Skiing

Cost: $60 ski-lift ticket, $300 assorted other gear.
Available: At ski areas at most mountain passes.

Supposedly the light reflected off the snow helps clear up the winter blues. Not for the budget minded, skiing is also thought to help depression by reaffirming the fact you are one of the social elite.

In-Home Tropical Paradise

Cost: $300 for plants, $300 for grow lights, $30 for Afro-Cuban CDs, $50 for patio furniture, $100 per month for electricity, $400 for one monkey (optional).
Available: Home Depot (except for monkey, which can be special-ordered).

Re-create a tropical jungle in your own home! Section off a room for your own personal paradise. Fill the whole room with large, tropical foliage. Arrange grow lights and patio furniture, crank up the heat, and turn on the music. If you opted for a monkey, dress it up as a waiter and have it serve you frosty drinks.

Positive Affirmations

Cost: $0.
Available: From the bowels of your subconscious mind.

Remember the scene in *Stand and Deliver,* when the kids are in an unair-conditioned classroom repeating, "Cool, cool, cool" over and over again? Same concept, but say, "Warm, warm, warm." Soon you'll be burning up. Other affirmations to try: "I am happy," "I'd marry me," and "The sun does exist."

Recommended Movies

The Shining: Don't let this happen to you.

Winter People: Watch Kurt Russell battle the elements.

Hard Rain: Christian Slater saves the day—even during a flood!

Seven: It never stops raining in this movie. Well, not until the box scene.

The Winter Guest: Emma Thompson and her mother go out on a cold day.

Blade Runner: It doesn't stop raining in the future, either!

The Ascent: Think it's cold here? Check out Russia during the winter and WWII!

Dead Man: Johnny Depp out West during the winter.

It's a Wonderful Life: It is?

Cold Fever: Japanese tourist in Iceland. Brrr.

Sleep: Andy Warhol shows you what you might look like all damn winter long.

Home for the Holidays: Jodie Foster tells it like it really is.

Fargo: They just might have it worse.

To Die For: Ice skating on an ice princess.

The Thing: Set in Antarctica. Not only is it cold, there's a crazy alien on the loose.

Recommended Books

Alive by Piers Paul Read: What do you do if you get trapped in your house by a blizzard? Pass the freeze-dried ass strips, please.

Call of the Wild by Jack London: Join a dog for a trip to Alaska. It's really cold up there, so you can't whine about a little rain.

Ice Storm by Rick Moody: When there's a storm in the Northeast, all hell breaks loose.

The Sweet Hereafter by Russell Banks: Snow equals bus crash; doesn't that suck?

Snow Falling on Cedars by David Guterson: It really *snows* on those islands?

A Perfect Storm by Sebastian Junger: Is there such a thing?

Into the Wild by John Krakauer: Let's hitchhike to Alaska and live in an unheated trailer!

Into Thin Air by John Krakauer: Let's climb the biggest mountain in the world and see who doesn't make it!

Isaac's Storm: A Man, a Time, and the Deadliest Hurricane in History by Erik Larson: Count your blessings.

War and Peace by Leo Tolstoy: It's going to be a very, very long winter.

Misery by Stephen King: Look out for big-boned fans.

Winters Without Snow by Colleen McElroy: She gets it.

Darkness at Noon by Arthur Koestler: Existential crisis, anyone?

Pitch Dark by Renata Adler: When she's not running down her friends at the *New Yorker,* Adler can write a dark piece of fiction.

Holidays on Ice by David Sedaris: Wow! Holidays *are* funny!

Holidaze Help

Besides the darkness and gloom, something even more sinister exists during December: holidays. Whether you are Jewish, Christian, or heathen, there are holidays that you must celebrate with your troubling family. Rules to make it through:

- Consume enormous amounts of alcohol or marijuana before stepping foot across the holly-decked/menorah-lit doorstep of your relatives.
- Borrow a small child or pet to bring with you: Living things like this create a wonderful distraction.
- At the dinner table, don't share your theory that Uncle Al is Satan.
- Only buy gifts you can afford. Places like the town dump or local 99-cent stores work well. Keep in mind your relatives will love to receive gifts like troll refrigerator magnets or airbrushed Virgin Mary wall clocks.
- Or, instead of just coping with someone else's gala, throw your own winter solstice party and insist your relatives come to *your* house, on *your* terms (see page 60).

Pagan Party Planner

So, you've decided to take control of your life—congratulations. As any new ager worth his or her crystal dust will tell you, those damn Christians stole the pagans' winter solstice celebration and renamed it Christmas. Take back that pagan holiday!

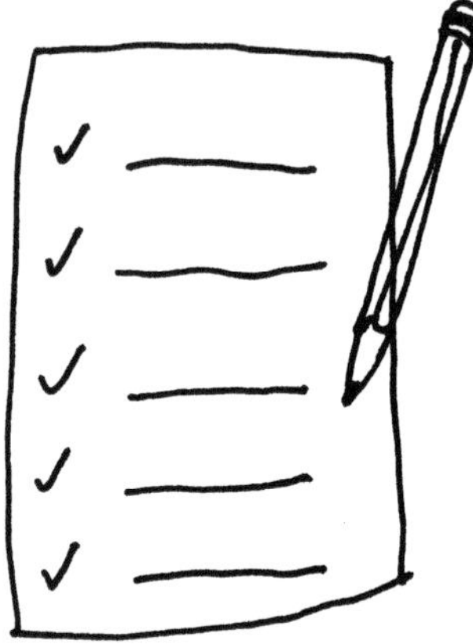

☐ **Invitations**

Send invites two weeks before the winter solstice. Invites should tell guests when (around December 21; consult your lunar calendar—what?! you don't have one?!!); where (in your backyard or a forest clearing); and what to wear (horns and furs). Think pagan when designing the invitations—use real pieces of leaf or bark, or maybe write the invites in blood.

☐ **Decorations**

Dress up your backyard or the local forest clearing with all the fixings that make pagans feel at home—an altar, candles, incense, bones, rocks, and other magical items. To stave off the darkness (and rodents), build a gigantic bonfire.

☐ Ice Breakers

You'll have to provide ice breakers to ensure everyone will mix, because your Uncle Joe probably doesn't know your best friend Jill. Why not have them become fast friends by having them slaughter a lamb together?

☐ Refreshments

Pagans were simple folk; offer simple drinks like grog, and snacks of fruit, bread, and roasted meats. You may choose to pass out consciousness-altering substances like psilocybin mushrooms, but keep in mind your aunt's bladder-control problems.

☐ Entertainment

All pagan rituals need a focal point—have each guest toss an offering into the fire (remember, it's more blessed-be to give than receive), and invite everyone to join in a ritual dance that involves writhing and groping. Pass out all manner of musical instruments—lutes, drums, nose flutes, kazoos—and encourage guests to play until dawn.

Top 10 Things to Do in the Dark

After daylight saving time ends, it gets preternaturally dark. What is one supposed to do during the hours after work and before bed? Or on those dark weekends?

⑩ Drink vodka.

⑨ Have a backyard bonfire/book-burning party.

⑧ Wear an extremely ugly clothing item—culottes, rope belt—and get away with it.

⑦ Stockpile lightbulbs.

⑥ Host a glowworms slumber party.

⑤ Perform satanic rituals/sacrifices in the backyard.

④ Peek through your neighbor's windows.

③ Look through your neighbor's trash.

② Download tropical island–themed porn.

① Paint your body with radioactive compounds, and marvel at that magical glow.

Northwest Weather Persona

Elvira Moody

Umbrella: Yes; velvet.

Winter gripe: Clove cigarette goes out in the rain.

Coping mechanism: Not necessary; enjoys darkness.

The night is celebrated by this dreary denizen. Plenty of dark clothes, ornate umbrellas, cowls, and magical powers keep her dry and snug. Who says velvet can't repel rain?

January: Sexual Healing

Average Low: 34°F
Average High: 45°F
Average Rainfall: 5.4"

1 in 5 Americans has been celibate for at least a year; 1 in 20 engages in sex at least every other day.

January

Sex and drinking are two things that go together, like *Sesame Street* and sponsorship. When it's summer, "sex on the beach" works as both a drink and as fantasy foreplay—but when it's midwinter and the sun bares itself in maliciously short fits, sex transforms into a burrowing, heat-seeking, German-term craving, like the need for wine with ice cream (the Germans do have a word for that, don't they?). You need something larger and more obliging in your bed than a heating pad. You need a . . .

Hibermate Defined

A "hibermate" is a term we here at BRITE have coined to mean someone you want to spend a lot of time with in the winter—someone whose body heat index (see Table B) rocks you off the charts and makes you think it's July in January.

If you already have a hibermate, January is the perfect time to rediscover the potential for warmth. We know you've gotten used to your side of the bed, but practice a little continental drift—snuggle up and dream about Bermuda. Having a fight about your icy-cold feet is sure to add a little spark to your relationship.

If you haven't yet found your hibermate, we're here for you. You need sex, and the search for sex is a good reason—maybe the only reason—to leave your house after dark in January. "But it's cold," we hear you say. "It's dark when I come home from work! My little black dress is sleeveless, for God's sake! I don't want to go out." But remember: January is the best time to find love. People will be drawn to you like heat-seeking missiles—you'll see. Picture this:

You walk into the restaurant and heat billows up around you, curling your hair like a rose vine. The lights are dim, casting a parchment glow against the richly colored walls—and then it happens! There, in the corner, your lover sits, chest heaving slightly, as if after a brisk run in chilly rain. Your eyes meet, and you swear there's the shock of static although you have yet to touch. Even as you walk toward the table, the waiter begins to pour a snifter of brandy, and the night unfolds like expensive flannel sheets, soon to be warmed by two very hot bodies.

You see? We know: You need help. You can't do it alone.

Assessing a Potential Hibermate

You must calculate the pros and the cons of each potential hibermate you meet. Take into consideration each one's body heat index score (see Table B) and come up with an appropriate pick-up line. Here are five sample hibermates; use this as a guide for others you may encounter.

Web Fortran

Occupation: Computer programmer.
Where to meet: Doesn't frequent bars—must seek him out at Sun Microsystems conventions, Star Trek chat rooms.
Pros: Easily convinced into bed.
Cons: Will insist you call a certain body part "Captain Picard," and will repeatedly yell, "Make it so!"
Body heat index rating: 45 units (but if he brings his computer along, could exceed 90!).
Best pick-up line to use: "Wanna come to my place and see my Apple Black Box?"
Tip: Web is a bit cold, but easily acquired. He may heat up after a game of D & D.

Larry LaBido

Occupation: "Personal trainer."
Where to meet: Singles bars.
Pros: Will convince *you* into bed.
Cons: Forgets your name, mostly just calls you "baby."
Body heat index rating: 350 units.
Best pick-up line to use: "Hello."
Tip: Repulsive, but *hot!* Close your eyes and pretend you're with someone you respect.

Ivana Di

Occupation: Mortuary attendant.
Where to meet: Cemeteries.
Pros: Into S&M.
Cons: Into S&M.
Body heat index rating: 100 units.
Best pick-up line to use: "Darling, I can hear your telltale heart."
Tip: She does seem a bit chilly at times, but remember: velvet sheets.

Grizzled Adams

Occupation: Survivalist.
Where to meet: Shooting range.
Pros: Lots of hair = more warmth!
Cons: He will request a new, larger hairdo on you (see the Farrah Fawcett, page 24).
Body heat index rating: 300 units.
Best pick-up line to use: "Are you packin' a 32-caliber, or are you just glad to see me?"
Tip: To increase his body heat index rating, ask him to bring you gifts of warm animal carcasses.

Ima Toorich

Occupation: Anything that nets more than $100,000 a year.
Where to meet: Posh health clubs.
Pros: She might buy you a fur coat.
Cons: You'll have to hide your piddly paycheck stubs.
Body heat index rating: 200 units in bed, up to 1,200 units on a bank floor strewn with money.
Best pick-up line to use: Scream, "Buy, buy!" into your cell phone. She will be drawn to you like a well-dressed moth to a wealthy flame.
Tip: If you're good enough, she'll take you to Bermuda.

The Dos and Don'ts of Winter Seduction

DO wear fur, real or fake. In caveman times, fur symbolized a rich winter larder—and we're not *that* evolved.

DON'T forget to shave. Wrong kinda fur, baby.

DO use a musky perfume or cologne. Musk is the smell of a warm, intimate space.

DON'T wear the same coat you wore skiing last weekend. Wrong kinda musk.

DO buy your potential hibermate a drink: Cognac or scotch is best.

DON'T buy a fancy drink that lights on fire. You don't want to be tacky, for god's sake.

DO put on some romantic music.

DON'T hum "Love and Marriage."

DO arrange candles artfully throughout the room (candlelight is more flattering than artificial light, and the most flattering angle is table-height).

DON'T set your bed on fire.

Buying Him or Her a Drink

Once you've picked out your potential hibermate, it's time to enter seduction mode. Your first step is to buy your target a drink. It's very important, however, to consider what kind of drink you're buying, because a drink says a lot about a person and what a person expects. To that effect, we have created the following:

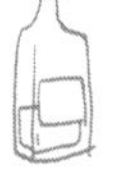

If You Buy Someone This:	You're Telling Them That:
Martini:	"I'm sophisticated."
Martini with two olives:	"I'm sophisticated and hungry."
Cosmopolitan:	"Hey, you're a big city girl/guy."
Kamikaze:	"I'm trying to get you drunk."
Tequila shot:	"I'm trying to get you drunk and take advantage of you."
Rum and Coke:	"I'm trying to get you drunk the same way I tried back at the frat house."
Red wine:	"I'm boring, but I can probably cook."
Champagne:	"I'm willing to spend large amounts of money on you."
White wine:	"I haven't dated since the '70s."

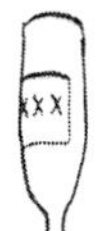

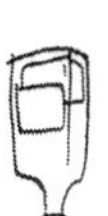

Table B: Body Heat Index

Specimen	Score
Male human, 200 pounds, with clothes on	50
Male human, 200 pounds with clothes off	75
Male human, 200 pounds with clothes off, after four vodka gimlets	300
Female human, 150 pounds with clothes on	50
Female human, 150 pounds with clothes off	75
Female human, 150 pounds with clothes off, after hearing the words, "I'd like to meet your mother"	500
Human baby	20,000
Large dog	30
Small dog/cat	15

Specimen	Score
Chicken	4.5
Small chicken	2.25
*Computer	45
*Hot water bottle	2.15
*Hot beverage in "travel mug"	1
*Hot beverage in to-go paper cup	0.02

*Although some of these items are not considered real "bodies" by experts, it could be argued, especially in a winter-catalyzed dementia, that things such as hot water bottles, computers, and beverages may be considered to be alive.

Warma Sutra

The Kama Sutra is the East Indian art devoted to enjoyment via the five senses—hearing, feeling, seeing, tasting, and smelling—assisted by the brain and the soul. But we are concerned with only one sense: feeling warm. To that end, we here at BRITE have created the Warma Sutra: positions that will allow you to be as warm as possible with your partner.

Foreplay

Embraces

When one partner clings to the other, just as ivy would around a tree, and bends his or her head down to hers or his with the desire of kissing, softly making cooing sounds, and they look lovingly toward one another, this is known as Blackberry Vine, an embrace like the twining of a creeper.

Sexual Embraces

When the lovers lie on the bed and embrace each other so closely that the arms and thighs of the one are encircled by the arms and thighs of the other, and they rub against each other, this is known as the Grizzly Bear, an embrace like the search for food in knapsacks.

Kissing

There is no fixed time or order between the embrace, the kiss, the pressing or scratching with the nails or fingers, but all these things should be done for warmth.

Positions

Positions for maximum warmth take their names from objects found in nature. You will find inspiration everywhere, even as we have.

- **Ducks Flying South**
  Locate the southern direction. Surround yourself with down comforters. Lie down with your partner's feet entwined in yours, so that your bodies approximate a V-shape with the point of the V facing south. Flap arms gently.

- **Rising Tides**
  Lie in bed with one partner's feet near the other partner's head. Tug covers back and forth throughout the night.

- **Rhododendron Blossom**
  Coat yourself and your partner with Bag Balm or petroleum jelly. Don fuzzy robes. Sleep with legs entwined.

- **Drunken Ferry Captain**
  Throughout the night, bump sterns repeatedly.

- **Totem Pole**
  One lover sits on the other lover's shoulders. Switch every 20 minutes. Invite others to join, if needed.

Baby Name Bonanza

OK, you've got a hibermate; let the mating begin! There's nothing warmer than a little bundle of joy (see Table B, Body Heat Index). But maybe you're having trouble coming up with an original name? We've all heard of a Mariah or known a Rain—why not use an exotic weather pattern?

- **Austru:** A west wind blowing over the lower Danube. Much better than Allan or Alex.
- **Bayamo:** A violent thunder squall on the south coast of Cuba, with gusty winds passing through the Sierra Maestra range. Wanted Ben, but that seemed boring.
- **Bhoot:** In India, a term describing a relatively small-scale counterclockwise whirling of air filled with loose dust.
- **Chergui:** Hot air that drifts into Morocco. Oh-so-much better than Cheryl.
- **Donner:** German for "thunder."
- **Etesian:** Cool air that blows across the Mediterranean Sea. More sonorous than Ethan.
- **Lung-wong:** The god of rain and wind in China.
- **Mammatus:** Similar to Manny but more fun! Clouds that look like pouches hanging from the undersides of other clouds.
- **Narai:** A cold Japanese wind.

- **Regnet:** German for rain; much better than Regis.
- **Seistan:** A good alternative for the hum-drum Steven, this is a wind in Iran that can blow for up to four months.
- **Taku:** Like Tammy but need something slightly different? Try this Alaskan word for wind.
- **Tramontana:** Considering Tracy? Why not try this one? Means a cool wind that blows over the western coast of Italy.
- **Virga:** Precipitation that falls from a cloud but evaporates before reaching the ground. Achingly beautiful!
- **Zonda:** Better than Vonda. A hot, enervating north wind that blows over Argentina's pampas.

Hibermate Scorecard

Most successful pick-up line:

Time elasped before you reached "Second Base":

Alcoholic beverage that made the other person seem more attractive than they actually are:

Highest approximate body heat temperature reached:

Methods used to obtain a sweltering body heat index:

Dumped them because:

Method of dumping that made you seem like a "good person":

Did You Do January Right?

(A Checklist)

- ☐ I went to a bar at 6 a.m.
- ☐ I predicted the body heat index of various bar patrons with 99% accuracy.
- ☐ I bought Larry La Bido a drink called "Sex on the Beach."
- ☐ I danced to the song "Love Cats" with Ivana Di.
- ☐ I played a ZZ Top song on the jukebox for Grizzled Adams.
- ☐ I pick-pocketed Ima Toorich.
- ☐ I weighed the pros and cons of picking up Web Fortran, and decided to pass.
- ☐ I came up with my own, original pick-up lines.
- ☐ I scored a red-hot hibermate by plying him/her with "Tequiza."
- ☐ I became a student of the erotic art of the Warma Sutra.
- ☐ My hibermate and I did the "Drunken Ferry Captain" position.
- ☐ My hibermate and I achieved a combined body heat index score of 900.
- ☐ I named my resultant baby "Bhoot."
- ☐ My baby has a body heat index score of 15,000.

Northwest Weather Persona

Betty Pager

Umbrella:
Lacroix, of course.

Winter gripe:
Vespa skids
in the rain.

Coping mechanism:
Listening to Devo.

This smart dresser is severely hindered by the rain and cold weather. Although she gets to wear fab caps and scarves, her coif does suffer.

February: Where to Find the Will to Live

Average Low: 36°F
Average High: 50°F
Average Rainfall: 4"

Most popular day to kill yourself: Monday

February

It's February, and you know what that rhymes with: dreary. Well, almost. Dreary February guarantees weeks of fuzzy gray days, where the sun merely snickers at us through cloud cover so dense it could rival congressional politics, and the thought of anything but sleep seems bewildering. Do you find yourself staring at the television all evening, wondering what the laugh track is supposed to be prompting? Do you answer the phone with a grunt? Can you muster only the faintest enthusiasm for exercise and—god forbid—sex? When someone tells you a joke, do you squint at this person as if he or she is speaking a foreign language? Are you sobbing as you read this paragraph, moaning, "When will it end? When, I ask you?"

Honey, either you need to put down this book or you are depressed. But don't worry—we here at BRITE are specially trained to deal with the psychological and psychosomatic effects of long stints of winter. We will share.

Case Study of Depression: Kevin & Dr. Blandenbot

Intensive laboratory studies on our voluntary test subject, Kevin, combined with sessions with Kevin's therapist, Dr. Blandenbot, have yielded valuable information about homeopathic and man-made chemical intervention.

Kevin is a 27-year-old male who finds himself unmotivated during the winter. He frequently spends long stretches watching reruns of *M.A.S.H.*, laughing hysterically at Klinger's effeminate getups. When his girlfriend, Darlene, points out that they haven't had sex in weeks, he says, "But I haven't seen this episode of *M.A.S.H.* in hours." He wears the same dingy sweats day in and day out, even when his employer reminds him that "it's not casual Tuesday." He eats only Ding Dongs, because "they come in shiny foil." Last week, he unearthed his Cure albums from high school, and he can occasionally be heard humming "Pictures of You." Kevin needs help.

At Darlene's urging, Kevin contacted Dr. Blandenbot, a specialist in SAD (look up there on his document-studded wall, and you can see his SAD diploma). SAD, which stands for Seasonal Affective Disorder, is a form of depression caused by low levels of natural light, and it makes people—you guessed it—sad. But sadness comes in many forms, and SAD sufferers seek solace in a variety of of bad television reruns, not just *M.A.S.H.* Dr. Blandenbot has seen patients complain of addiction to *Married with Children, The Cosby Show,* and, quite commonly among Generation Xers, *The Brady Bunch.* Dr. Blandenbot says Kevin may want to watch *M.A.S.H.* because "it symbolizes the war internally, the real war between dark and light—the seasonal darkness and lightness that can only be treated externally."

Dr. Blandenbot has urged Kevin to keep a diary, recording significant and meaningful events of each day. Following are excerpts:

February 7

6 a.m.: Couldn't sleep. Found *M.A.S.H.* on channel 64. The episode where Hawkeye and Hotlips get trapped beneath ground while on reconnaissance. They kiss. Made me sleepy.

11 a.m.: At work. Tried to engage colleagues in detailed discussion of the psychological implications of Radar's teddy-bear fetish. Found myself alone, in bathroom, sobbing.

February 10

6 a.m.: Found *M.A.S.H.* on channel 64 again. Fell asleep to closing credits, murmuring about power outage.

7 p.m.: Darlene discovered Ding Dongs supply. Tried to explain to her that Ding Dongs represent sunshine, both in shape and wrapping reflectivity. She threw them away, but I have more hidden behind cat box.

february 14

6 p.m.: Presented Darlene with Ding Dongs cake, carefully crafted out of 16 Ding Dongs. She refused to eat it, claiming it smelled like cat poop. Drank three beers.

11:30 p.m.: *M.A.S.H.* episode where Klinger and Father Mulcahey find the stolen penicillin hidden under the church bell. Coincidence?

february 22

8 a.m.: Darlene awoke me with a kiss. I heard rain outside and rolled over.

11:30 p.m.: The episode where the Colonel dies. Ah, Henry Blake. I thought about my own death—will it be so notable?

february 26

4 a.m.: I was awake for the dreams episode of *M.A.S.H.*, in which Hawkeye has a nightmare about floating mannequin limbs. Found myself disinterested.

3 p.m.: At work, I dozed off during the boss's motivational speech and was sent to the copy room in disgrace. Ate my spare Ding Dongs.

Symptoms of Depression

As you can see, Kevin exhibits one or more of the typical symptoms of clinical depression:

- ☐ Inability to sleep, or desire to sleep all the time
- ☐ Loss of sexual function
- ☐ Decrease in appetite, or increase in appetite
- ☐ Pessimism, lethargy, feelings of worthlessness
- ☐ Restlessness and irritability
- ☐ Headaches, stomachaches, backaches, muscle and joint pain
- ☐ Junk food and/or alcohol binging
- ☐ Use of mood-altering drugs
- ☐ Heedless risky behavior
- ☐ Thoughts of death or self-inflicted pain

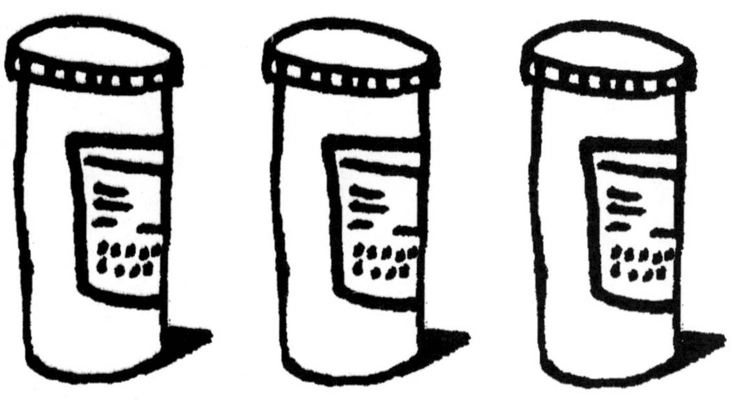

Are You Depressed? [A Quiz]

Just as it is very difficult to find your glasses when you're not wearing them, the conundrum of depression is that you can't really see it when you're in the middle of it. You may wonder why it suddenly takes you two hours to get out of bed in the morning, or how that large chocolate cake in the fridge suddenly disappeared. You need to figure out just how depressed you are—if you are indeed depressed—to plan a path of resistance. Therefore, BRITE has put together this little questionnaire:

❶ **Much of the time, do you feel:**

Ⓐ Like the sad clown in that Judy Collins song?

Ⓑ As though the only real insight can be found on TV?

Ⓒ As worthless as a sock with no partner?

❷ **Much of the time, do you:**

Ⓐ Have difficulty deciding whether to watch *The Simpsons* or *Third Rock from the Sun*?

Ⓑ Have trouble figuring out what the commercials are supposed to be selling?

Ⓒ Forget what just happened on your favorite sitcom?

❸ **Lately, have you:**

Ⓐ Lost interest in the latest developments on *Jeopardy*?

Ⓑ Had problems at work because you can only talk about television?

Ⓒ Isolated yourself from others and fantasized about your love life with Katie Couric?

❹ **Lately, have you:**

Ⓐ Not had enough energy to search for the remote and been stuck watching *Frasier*?

Ⓑ Yelled irritably at the latest perfume commercial?

Ⓒ Fallen asleep with your head on Ding Dongs?

❺ **Lately, have you:**

Ⓐ Wandered to the corner store for more Ding Dongs, wearing only your underwear?

Ⓑ Stuffed Ding Dongs into your cheek pouches "for later"?

Ⓒ Found yourself staring at seven empty beer bottles?

If you read and answered every question, you aren't depressed but most likely have an addiction to answering quizzes in self-help books. Enroll in psychotherapy. If you

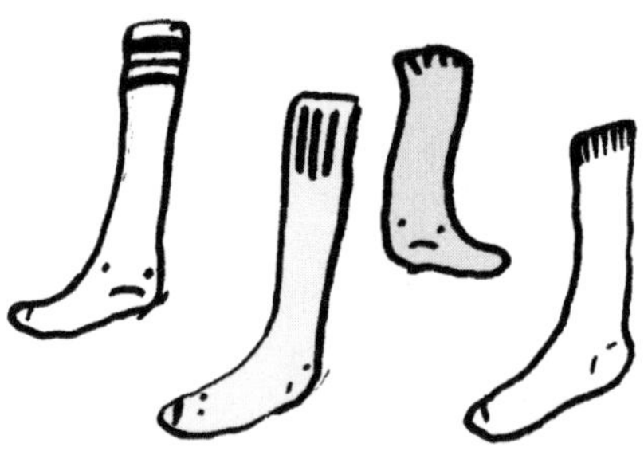

skipped this quiz entirely, you may be in denial and could be suffering from depression. Seek medical attention. If you read one question and skipped to the answers, you're mildly depressed but can manage it with self-medication. Proceed to Drugstore.com.

I'd Like You to Meet My New Best Friend: Drugstore.com

Yeah, there's your therapy, there's your talk-talk-talk, but why not skip to the real thing? Drugs. According to authorities, "antidepressant medications successfully elevate mood in 60 percent to 80 percent of people who use them as directed for a time span of several months."

Depression is physically based in these things called neurotransmitters in your brain. Neurotransmitters are chemicals that carry messages from one nerve cell to another. The gaps between nerve cells are called synapses. When one cell releases neurotransmitters, its nerve impulse is carried to the next cell, like a really good piece of gossip. Then special enzymes (called, perhaps, Martha Stewart enzymes) clear away the neurotransmitter so the next one can be sent without interference.

People who are depressed have lower levels of certain neurotransmitters: serotonin, epinephrine, norepinephrine, and dopamine. Some antidepressants interfere with the enzymes that clean up (take *that*, Martha Stewart enzymes!), so more neurotransmitters remain; others act on specific neurotransmitters.

So all you have to do is match up your neurotransmitters to the appropriate drug, right? It may take a little experimentation, but in the interest of science we here at BRITE took our test subject, Kevin, on a tour of antidepressants. This is what we learned.

The "Guide to Antidepressants" Guide

- ☐ **Buspar**
  Acts on autoreceptor subtype 5-HT1A. Will not cloud the intellect. A good, basic, all-around antidepressant.

  Kevin, after six weeks: "Boring."

- ☐ **Paxil**
  Part of the family of SSRIs (selective serotonin reuptake inhibitors), Paxil promises to brighten mood and reduce anxiety.

  Kevin, after six weeks: "Hey, this isn't too bad."

- ☐ **Zoloft**
  Zoloft is also an SSRI, promising fewer side effects than the older drugs.

  Kevin, after six weeks: "You know what we should do? We should redecorate this place. I mean, that lamp is really '80s—and the desk there, in the corner? Sterile. Move it here, under the window, and paint this wall kind of a sea green . . ."

- ☐ **Prozac**
  Prozac gained notoriety in the early '90s as a wonder drug. While some people touted its livening effects, others complained that it flattened out experience. It continues to be popular with psychiatrists.

  Kevin, after six weeks: "No, it's OK. I'm happy to just sit here. Look at that magnolia outside. It's really

beautiful, isn't it? No, I know I said I'd like some tea, but it's really OK."

- [ ] **Amineptine (Wellbutrin)**
A selective dopamine reuptake blocker. Higher doses of this drug have been reported to cause spontaneous orgasm. It is fast-acting.

Kevin, after six weeks: "Uhhhhhhh."

- [ ] **Hypericum (St. John's Wort)**
A natural alternative to over-the-counter medicines, hypericum appears to effectively brighten mood and lessen anxiety. It is important to know the appropriate dosage, however.

Kevin, after six weeks: "Give me the Wellbutrin."

- [ ] **Chocolate**
Some people claim that chocolate not only brightens moods, but works as an aphrodisiac as well. So we decided to try it on Kevin.

Kevin, after six weeks: "Hello! Wellbutrin! Can anybody hear me?

Weather Astrology

What does your sign say about your reaction to the Northwest weather?

Aries: March 20—April 18

OK, control tower, we know you've got it all figured out–stockpiling for winter, how to weatherize your house, weather-predicting methods using only a stick of gum and a toothpick. And you certainly know how to have fun doing such things as skiing and storm watching–but try to avoid bragging; nobody else wants to hear about it.

Ideal hibermate sign: Gemini

Taurus: April 19—May 20

If you were Santa, you'd probably get all of the children's presents delivered by, oh, April. Similarly, you don't buy an umbrella until just after the Fourth of July, sunglasses until November. You are able to enjoy many aspects of the weather, including the feeling of raindrops and foggy mornings. You make the best snow angels ever.

Ideal hibermate sign: Cancer

Gemini: May 21—June 20

Rain or drizzle, you keep smiling. And talking. What better thing, Gemini, to discuss but the weather? And it keeps changing, just like your opinions. You also enjoy planning for every disaster that could take place—leave it to the twins to buy 20-pound sacks of salt for the entire block's sidewalks and a backhoe for scraping out your driveway.
Ideal hibermate sign: Aries

Cancer: June 21—July 22

During a rainstorm, you hand out umbrellas and hot tea; summertime, you make mint juleps and rub sunscreen on everyone's back. You are the sign most susceptible to getting SAD during the dark winters, so find a hibermate pronto!
Ideal hibermate sign: Taurus

Leo: July 23—August 22

You don't mind wearing a rubber jumpsuit during the rainy season, and the tiniest bathing suit during the summer. In fact, you expect massive adoration for your fashion eccentricities. If anyone tries to remind you about the awful rubber rash you acquired or the third-degree sunburn you got from last year's thong, deny it.
Ideal hibermate sign: Aquarius

Virgo: August 23—September 22

Hand-embroidered snow scenes on your winter jacket? Waterproofed your high heels? Polished your umbrella? Only you, Virgo, can find time for the small but oh-so-important details during the depressing winter. But don't be disappointed if everyone else isn't as fastidious as you are—and please, don't lecture them about it.
Ideal hibermate sign: Pisces

Libra: September 23—October 22

If anyone can convince the clouds to go away, or order away the rain, you can, Libra—face it, you are a natural charmer. But you might not want to use this charm, recognizing that without the protective cloud cover, people might get a painful sunburn, or without rain, the grass would not be so green.
Ideal hibermate sign: Sagittarius

Scorpio: October 23—November 21

Poor Scorp, your moods will follow the changes of the weather no matter what you do—you'll be dark and gloomy during the winter, manic during the spring, and sunny and happy in the summer. And, sadly, there's no one to blame—resist the urge to fire your gun up into the clouds or make crank phone calls to the weather forecaster. Maybe you should take a long vacation in January.

Ideal hibermate sign: Capricorn

Sagittarius: November 22—December 21

You are more likely to ask, "Why does it rain?" than "When will it stop raining?" You enjoy the opportunity to ponder life's mysteries during the long winters. You will procrastinate necessary tasks like chopping wood and buying extra socks, though. And being the exaggerator that you are, when a dusting of snow lies on the ground, you'll be the first and only to use the word "blizzard."

Ideal hibermate sign: Libra

Capricorn: December 22—January 19

You can chop wood for longer than anyone else. You can knit the longest, thickest scarf. Your chicken soup will cure any illness—so get to it, Capricorn, and do what you do best. Take some time out from your various productions to enjoy your labors, and remember that everything doesn't have to be a competition.
Ideal hibermate sign: Scorpio

Aquarius: January 20—February 18

You're a rebel: You wear shorts in the winter, down jackets during the summer. And not just any shorts—gold lamé shorts. And not just any down jacket—a special emu down jacket. You have many ideas about how to survive a Northwest winter and will tell anyone with the brains to listen to you.
Ideal hibermate sign: Leo

Pisces: February 19—March 19

Just because you dream about a beach doesn't mean it's going to be sunny in November. You are extremely sensitive to shifts in weather patterns and tend to take it all just a bit too personally. For god's sake, it isn't raining because you're feeling sad! And we're afraid to report that no matter how hard you wish the sun would come out, it probably won't.
Ideal hibermate sign: Virgo

Winter Doldrums: Not Just a Weather Pattern

Many people experience a loss of sex drive during the winter. Here are five steps guaranteed to break through those winter doldrums:

Step ① Rearrange bedroom according to feng shui for lovers.

Step ② Rent and watch *9½ Weeks*.

Step ③ Put Barry White's *Is This Watcha Want?*—especially track 3, "I'm Qualified to Satisfy You"—on replay.

Step ④ Lie naked together on a bearskin rug.

Step ⑤ Lick each other's earlobes.

Northwest Weather Persona

X. Stacey

Umbrella: Yes; metallic silver.

Winter gripe: Baggy pants get soaked at the bottom.

Coping mechanism: Rave till dawn.

She's so far into trance and jungle music, she doesn't even know what season it is anyway. Since all the raves start once night falls, winter is actually prime season.

March: A Light at the End of the Tunnel

Average Low: 38°F
Average High: 54°F
Average Rainfall: 4"

Number of college students who travel to warm locations for spring break: 5 million*

March

*Number of those who will consume the beverage "Tequiza" and deeply offend the local population: 4.999 million

For the first time since November, you're getting your hopes up. The rain seems to be . . . could it be . . . lessening? The sun seems like a real thing again, not just a fever dream. The wind seems merely like something you could fly a kite in. Slap on that hat, baby, 'cause it's Springtime! The only month with a verb for a name, March can hit you like a virus. This reaction is so common that there's a term for it: Spring Fever. Although there are pop songs that refer to this phenomenon, Spring Fever is not to be taken lightly. This is a vulnerable time for you.

Symptoms That Determine If You Have Spring Fever

- Inability to cease gazing out the window (remember elementary school?).
- Tendency to pause, grinning, at the sound of birdsong.
- Tendency to *whistle along with* birdsong.
- Desire to leave the house without a coat at the slightest provocation (e.g., neighbor's floodlight that mimics a sunbreak), and to refuse to admit you're cold even when shivering so violently that you can't hold a to-go cup of coffee.
- Desire to hum any show tune having to do with the weather (e.g., "Singing in the Rain," "Tomorrow").
- Sudden tendency to flirt with baristas, bike messengers, elevator passengers, telephone solicitors, traffic cops, etc.
- Renewed interest in the seven-day forecast.

How to Survive Spring Fever

All right, so you have Spring Fever. It's not such a big deal! Stick with these guidelines and you'll be OK.

① Do not try to wear flip-flops for another three weeks. Your coordination won't be up to par until then, and you may get toe cramps.

② Clean sunglasses that have been sitting in the drawer for six months. Otherwise, you may think you've been stricken with myopia.

③ Do not flirt with public figures—it's potentially embarrassing.

④ Forbid yourself from thinking that people you work with are eligible dating material.

⑤ Repeat to yourself: "'Tomorrow' is a dumb song."

⑥ Don't trust the seven-day forecast.

Another reality check for those stricken with Spring Fever is to face the fact that it's still gonna rain. It's a good idea, when one becomes too giddy in March, to remember the old saying, "April showers bring May flowers." Beware: It's not even April yet! In fact, March gets just as much precipitation as February. The only difference is that it's a little bit warmer.

But, don't despair! The rain can be your friend! The rain brings you rainbows, and toadstools, and softer skin! It washes away the scum of the city! It's like an outdoor shower!

Oh, never mind.

Ways to Keep Out the Rain

The rain is notorious for seeping into any and all facets of supposedly "weather-proof" gear. We spend whole salaries on Gore-Tex, entire Christmas bonuses on Scotch-Guard, and still that one infernal drop manages to sneak through. So how do you manage?

Saran Wrap

We know, you're thinking this sounds like January, the sex chapter—but you don't need to cover yourself completely in this convenient element to benefit from it. Merely wrap appropriate amounts over your wrists, where your sleeves meet your hands, and around your ankles, and you're airtight.

Duct Tape

Similarly, duct tape is quite a remarkable water-blocking material. And even more handy, when you're done using it, it functions to remove body hair very effectively.

Bathtub and Anti-Slip Decals

Those textured rubber stickers—so popular in the '70s—aid in gripping wet surfaces. Why not take advantage of them on wet days, too? You may apply them to the bottoms of your boots, to the elbows of your raincoat—even to the feet of your briefcase, so it stays put when you're waiting curbside for a cab.

Baseball Hat + CD JewelCase

This tip is a little trickier. Take a sturdy baseball cap and Scotch-Guard it. Now, open a CD case, break the thinner front pane off it, and, using a heavy-gauge thread, sew it so that it hangs from the baseball cap like a windshield. For an added practical element, spray your "windshield" with anti-fog.

Laminated Newspaper

It's ever-so-fashionable when it's raining to cross the street clutching your briefcase in one hand and holding a folded newspaper over your head with the other. The only problem is, the newspaper inevitably degrades to a sodden pulp. So why not laminate it? Pick the edition of a special day—your birthday, maybe—and laminate it so that it still folds tabloid-wise. Carry it with you at all times.

Remembering Our Differences: Hats Are from Mars, Umbrellas Are from Venus

One day, Hat Wearers looked over and saw Umbrella Carriers. The Umbrella Carriers and Hat Wearers were drawn to each other. They were happy together, until a major storm broke loose from the skies. During the storm, the Hat Wearers complained about how the umbrella kept inverting in the wind, and the Umbrella Carriers complained about how the Hat Wearer's head smelled weird.

If the Hat Wearers and Umbrella Carriers aren't aware that they are *supposed* to be different, they will be at odds with each other. Let's examine the differences.

Life with the Hat On

Hat Wearers value compactness, wind resistance, and warmth, and don't mind getting a little wet.

Life Under the Umbrella

Umbrella Carriers have different values. They, under no condition, want their hair or body to contact moisture. In most ways, their world is the opposite of the Hat Wearers.

How the Hat Wearers and Umbrella Carriers Found Peace

They recognized each other's differences. Hat Wearers forgave Umbrella Carriers for poking them in the eye, and Umbrella Carriers forgave Hat Wearers for their messy hairdos. Now they are living happily ever after.*

*Truth be told, more Umbrella Carriers will buy in to this highly marketed idea than Hat Wearers. And Umbrella Carriers will insist on reading these pages aloud to the Hat Wearers and saying, "See, see, get it? Get it? We're different!" This will only widen the yawning gap that exists between them.

Chicken Soup for the Sodden

Perhaps your spirits are a little . . . dampened right now. Yes, it's going to rain, at least for one more month, but you can deal with it! To help you, here are some stories to warm your heart beneath the chilly Gore-Tex.

My Grandpa's Umbrella

My grandpa used to have a really big umbrella. When I visited him on rainy days, we'd huddle beneath it and walk to the library. He never told me where he got it, but it had the word "Corona" on it in really big letters. When he died, he left it to me in his will, saying, "I won't be needing this where I'm going."

The Lady on the Bus

It was a rainy day, and Jenny had been waiting at the bus stop for a while. When she got on the bus, there was nowhere to sit and she felt like crying. But then this really nice lady said, "Here, take my seat," and Jenny did.

The Puddle

Carrie had been waiting for what seemed like hours for the signal to change so she could cross the street. The corner where she stood was surrounded by a big puddle of water, but she didn't think much about it. Then a car came rushing by and splashed the puddle all over her. Muddy water dripped from her hair, from her nose, down her neck. Fortunately the cute guy standing next to her said, "I love a woman in mud," and they got married six months later.

The Crocus

It had been a long, hard winter. When I stepped out onto my front lawn, all I could see were dead brown plants. Slimy grass covered with rotting leaves bled out onto the pavement. "This is terrible," I thought. Then I saw a spot of color at the far end of the lawn. "A crocus!" I said. With a smile in my heart, I walked to where I could see it better. I bent down, and realized it was a wrapper from Taco Time, moldering in the worm-caked earth. "Oh, well," I said to myself. "Maybe next time."

Uncle Bob's Feather Boa

I always knew my Uncle Bob was special. When I went over to his house, I got to play with his glittery makeup and drink milk out of his high-heeled shoe, and it was our special secret. He wore girdles because he had a bad back. One time we were going to the park and it was really cold. I said, "But Uncle Bob, I don't think my coat is warm enough," and he pulled out a big yellow feather boa from his closet for me to wear. He said, "Now, don't tell your mom." And I never did. Until right now. Mom?

Submit Your Own Chicken Soup for the Sodden Story

Share your inspirational story with our readers!

What a Chicken Soup for the Sodden Story IS:

A Chicken Soup for the Sodden Story IS a true, motivational, inspiring, heartwarming, and heartfelt story about making it through another damp, miserable, ass-kicking Northwest winter!

What a Chicken Soup for the Sodden Story ISN'T:

It's NOT a term paper, a piece of debris that you found on the ground outside the courthouse, a parking ticket, or your high school transcripts.

Many of the stories and poems that you have read in the Chicken Soup for the Sodden series were submitted by readers like you. The simplest way to submit your story is by following these simple steps:

1. Write your story, making sure to include buzzwords like mud, rain, hail, feather boa, etc.

2. Send it to us, along with a small, one-time reading fee of $50, care of:

> Chicken Soup for the Sodden
> Cell Block 9543
> Walla Walla State Penitentiary
> Walla Walla, WA

Umbrella Factoids

- About 12 million people buy umbrellas every year.
- Stores in Seattle stock umbrellas four times as often as in other parts of the country.
- The Gustbuster umbrella can withstand 60-mile-an-hour winds.
- The Pocket Wonder umbrella weighs only 6 ounces, and when closed measures only 7.3 inches.

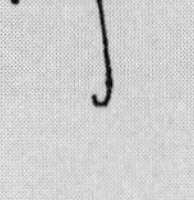

- Cost of a custom-made umbrella that houses a 15-inch glass whiskey flask in its malacca wood-handled shaft: $350.
- 43 percent of adult women don't use umbrellas.
- Weight of one of the 3,100 umbrellas lined along a Los Angeles highway in an art installation by the artist Christo: 435 pounds.

- Number of people killed by Christo's umbrellas: 2

Northwest Weather Persona

Allen Ginseng

Umbrella: No; naturally secreted oils repel rain.

Winter gripe: Too cold to go barefoot in the streets.

Coping mechanism: Poetry and coffee.

This resident actually likes the weather; he's always depressed anyway. The endless rainy season allows him to stay indoors pecking away at his manual typewriter, creating haiku about puddles and mud. Warning: Strange odors emitted when dampened.

April: Twelve Steps to Springtime Re-emergence

Average Low: 41°F
Average High: 59°F
Average Rainfall: 2.5"

Brightness of indoor lighting: 100–600 lux; brightness outdoors, even when overcast: 1,000–10,000 lux

April

April—the word trips off your tongue like a raindrop: *ape-rilll-ll.* Suddenly all that was sodden seems light as sea foam, all that was chilly takes on a gleam of sweet green. You find yourself peeling back one sweater, revealing one ear tip, undoing that top button—and the feel of air against your skin can be as invigorating as a manhandled loofah. Visions of hopping on your bicycle and taking a spin around the block fill your head. Visions of walking a long, sugar-sandy beach, dabbling your toes in surf that isn't iced over, tease your winter-addled brain.

But don't get on that bicycle just yet. Before you take that first step outside, pause for a moment. Look at yourself. Do your socks match? Are you wearing socks? Is that sweater-beneath-a-sweater really supposed to be bouclé, or is it actually covered in dime-sized lint? When you take off your long underwear, do your thighs themselves look a little baggy? Do you really think you can pass that bed head off as a fashion statement?

Just like the groundhog, you don't want to scare yourself on your first outing after winter. Think how much better it would be if you could sail out in style, ensuring six more weeks of sunny receptions. You need to get it together.

Northwesterners don't know how to deal with sunny weather when it happens. Seattlites buy more pairs of sunglasses per capita than the residents of any other city in the nation—not because we need them, obviously, but because we *lose* them all the time. We throw our arms out the car window screaming for a sunburn, we hustle to the beach forgetting to shave our armpits, we horrify visitors to our city by peering directly into the hazy circle of the sun, keening, "What is that glowing orb up in the sky?"

Are You Ready to Re-emerge?

❶ When you try on your swimsuit and look at yourself in the mirror, do you:

Ⓐ Fall on the floor writhing with laughter.

Ⓑ Run from the mirror as if your eyes have been blinded by a searchlight.

Ⓒ Whistle and strut.

❷ When you rub your palms against the bottom of your feet, do you:

Ⓐ Immediately call the emergency room because your hands have a callus burn.

Ⓑ Decide to take up tap dancing because your nails are so long they click on the floor.

Ⓒ Grasp your petal-soft feet and rub them ecstatically.

❸ When you put on some Chap Stick and wait five minutes, your lips:

Ⓐ Curl off in tiny bits like a pastry flake.

Ⓑ Are so dry they absorb the Chap Stick like a five-year-old with Kool-Aid.

Ⓒ Glisten like Mariah Carey's eyeshadow.

❹ When you twist your backside around to the mirror and give your butt a little slap, does this:

Ⓐ Set off an uncontrollable jiggling that travels in a jolly fashion from one buttock to another.

Ⓑ Make you feel as if you're participating in an ill-conceived amateur baby boomer "Do the Twist" competition.

Ⓒ Merely accentuate your lissome thighs and nipped-in waistline.

❺ When you feel your elbows (don't try to look at them! just feel them), are they:

Ⓐ Porous and chalky like a toasted English muffin.

Ⓑ Rough and slick like the peel of a grapefruit.

Ⓒ Soft like a bunny rabbit's nose.

If you answered Ⓐ and/or Ⓑ to any or all of these questions, you should feel lucky—fate is giving you a wake-up call. If you answered Ⓒ to any or all of these questions, you are either in delusional denial or you are clearly not of the human race; you should go back to your disgustingly perfect little planet and leave the rest of us to purchase beauty products in peace. For you Ⓐs and Ⓑs, though you have accepted yourselves as you are, now it is time to change.

The 12 Steps to Re-emergence

In order to help you learn about re-emergence, BRITE has compiled **12 Easy Steps.** Repeated as a credo, these steps aid the winter-sufferer in remembering what the summer sun is all about. All together, now:

Step 1: We admit that we are powerless over winter and that our lives will become unmanageable, incredibly messy, and despondently unfashionable.

Step 2: We will come to believe that a Power greater than ourselves (but NOT Martha Stewart) can restore us to sanity.

Step 3: We will make a decision to turn our will and our lives over to sun care, skin care, and to spring as we understand it.

Step 4: We will make a searching and fearless moral inventory of our spring wardrobe.

Step 5: We will admit to ourselves and to another human being the exact nature of our spring wardrobe.

Step 6: We are entirely ready to have a shopping expert remove all these defects of character.

Step 7: We will humbly ask a doctor or shopping consultant to remove our shortcomings.

Step 8: We will make a list of all persons we have harmed, such as those whose weddings we had attended dressed in black burlap, and are willing to make amends (cookies, sunscreen) to them all.

Step 9: We will make direct amends to such people wherever possible, except when to do so would injure them or others.

Step 10: We will continue to take personal inventory and when we are flabby or have terrible taste in our spring wardrobe, we promptly will admit it.

Step 11: We will seek, through short excursions outdoors, in less and less clothing each time, and through meditation and fasting, to improve our conscious contact with the sun as we understand it, praying only for knowledge of SPFs and for the power to carry that out.

Step 12: Having had a spiritual awakening as the result of these steps, we will try to bring this message to the sun-deprived and winter-weary, and will practice these principles in all our affairs.

Will There Be Rain?

In April, whether it will rain or not can be an exciting guessing game. But to take some of the guesswork out, try some of these prediction techniques. We don't promise they'll work, but we know a couple of old wives who think they will.

- ☐ Will it rain? Take your best umbrella—the really big, awkward one—with you when you go to work. We guarantee that'll keep it from raining.
- ☐ Wear your most expensive suede shoes. That will guarantee rain.
- ☐ Break a thumb-width bunch of spaghetti noodles in half. Scatter them on the deck. Turn around twice. Pick up the bunch. Are they slightly sticky? It will rain. Did they remain dry? It will drizzle.
- ☐ In the middle of the night, look up at the moon. If it has a halo around it, it will rain the next day. Either that, or you need to clean your contacts.
- ☐ If your dog eats grass, it will rain that day—unless he comes inside and vomits it up, in which case it'll be sunny for the 10 minutes you spend cleaning up the carpet.
- ☐ If the weather forecaster says there's a 50/50 chance of rain, it will rain. Duh.
- ☐ Take a dollar bill and fold it in half. Now fold it in half again. Now look at the half in front of you. If you can see an "o" on it, it will rain.

A Slightly Superstitious Forecasting Guide

- ☐ Get an old empty wine bottle, set it on an uncarpeted floor, and give it a spin. If it rests facing due east, it will rain. If it rests due west, it will rain. If it rests due south, it will rain a lot. If it rests due north, you'll have an afternoon of sunbreaks.
- ☐ Get a full bottle of wine and empty it into your mouth. Rain, sun—who cares?

Re-emergence Journal

Do not be discouraged. No one among us will always remember where we last put our sunglasses, or that culottes aren't in this year, or to put sunscreen even on our ear tips. We must take these steps one day at a time, sunbreak by subreak, as the month of April opens into May, then June and July. We must take quiet time to reflect on the meaning of the ugly bulb sprouting into the beautiful tulip. Remember: Always walk toward the light. Use this journal to help yourself stay on your primrose path.

I now realize that the areas of my body that are not re-emerging are:

____

____

____

____

____

____

____

____

____

____

____

____

____

____

____

____

I realize I find it difficult to re-emerge from the house when:

When I was able to re-emerge, I felt:

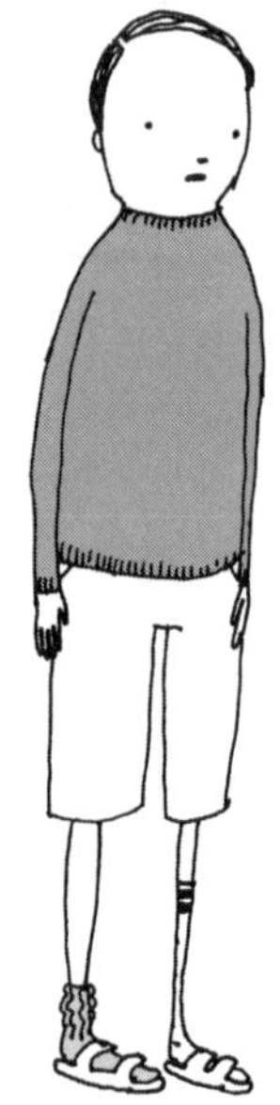

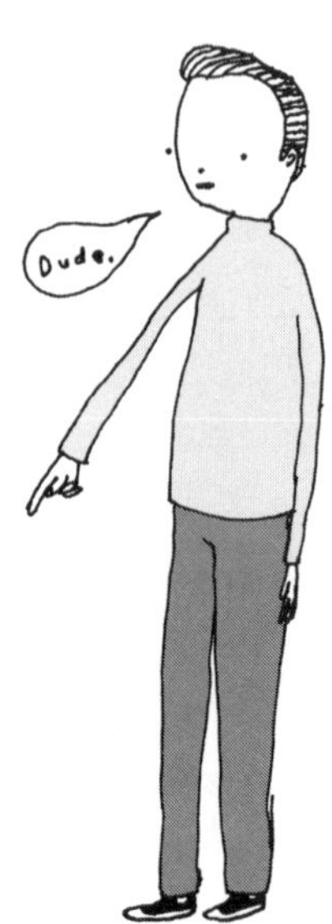

Buddy Up

Finding a buddy is one of the goals of the 12-step program. Buddies are good for helping you put on sunblock, for telling you when your sunglasses are perched on top of your head where you can't find them, and for sitting with you at outdoor cafes. After taking stock of your winter-addled life up to this point, you may be thinking, "Buddy? My *cats* don't want to be near me, why would another human being?" But take heart—your cats may be standoffish merely because you're not quite as furry now as you were all winter. Other human beings will appreciate this lack of fur, believe us.

The Buddy Creed

Once you find a buddy, you should take the buddy creed. The buddy creed is like a blood pact—so important, so vital to national friendship intelligence, that it has gone unpublished until now. Here it is:

"I, [state your name], do hereby swear to seek out new and televised beauty products for my buddy, to check my buddy's shoes for doggie doo, to note when weird things fall out of trees onto my buddy's hair, to assist my buddy through the final stages of automatic car washes, to tell my buddy when s/he's watching TV that's not funny, to alert my buddy when a potential date is making come-hither faces in a dark bar, and to point out whether the potential date really isn't very attractive but it's only the dark that makes him/her seem so."

A Good Buddy Should Be

1. Someone who is honest. Your buddy should not be too shy to tell you, "Oh, my God! Your socks are *two different colors!*"
2. Someone who shares the same shoe size.
3. Someone who knows the basic tenets of fashion, and who can tell you if your windbreaker is "*so* Y2K."
4. Someone—obviously—who is not afraid to speak in italics.
5. Someone who understands your taste in potential mates and respects it, but *does not share it.*
6. Someone who knows where all the good clubs are.

Buddy Bonding

It's good to have projects to do with your buddy so the two of you become closer. Trips to the mall aside, projects might include assessing weather trends with an amateur weather balloon (share the costs), re-caulking the sunroof on said friend's car, or inventing bumper-sticker phrases.

Re-emergence Aptitude Test

Finally, in order to evaluate your re-emergence readiness, BRITE suggests you take the following, patented Re-emergence Aptitude Test (RAT). It's just like the SAT, but way more important.

Metaphors

Springtime, just like a bad poem, is rife with metaphors. It's the time of year when you can look around, and almost any natural object is beaming you a special message about your current state of mind. Melting snowpacks? Fat melting from your thighs! Tulips? Your new nail-polish color! Tiny chirruping birds? Your après-cold voice!

To get you thinking more positively, here's a little metaphor/simile game you can play. Remember these from the SATs? An X is to Y as Z is to BLANK, with you filling in the blank. Here's an example:

Hair : Bird's Nest :: Teeth : Mossy Boulders

Now you try some.

Easter Bunny : Naked Mole Rat :: Your ex-boy/girlfriend :

____

Cat : Shedding Fur :: You : Shedding :

____

Rain Boots : Fashion :: Milton Berle :

____

Dampness : Polyester :: Mudslide :

____

Humidity : New Hairdo :: Half-ton Truck :

____

Mud Puddle : Passing Traffic :: Magnet :

____

Multiple Choice:

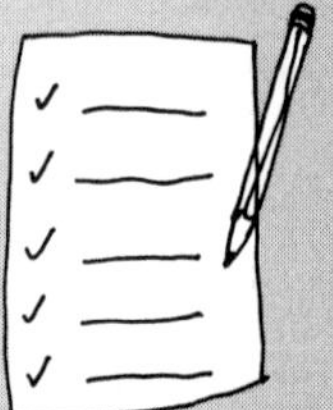

❶ How big are raindrops?

Ⓐ About as big as your thumb

Ⓑ Generally less than 1/50 inch in diameter

Ⓒ Depends on how small your raincoat is

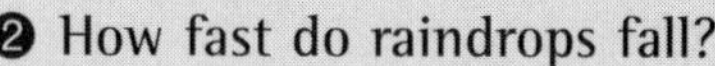

❷ How fast do raindrops fall?

Ⓐ 20 miles per hour

Ⓑ 7 miles per hour

Ⓒ Depends on how far away your car is

❸ What is the difference between drizzle and rain?

Ⓐ Two *z*'s and an *n*

Ⓑ Drizzle droplets are less than 1/50 inch in diameter

Ⓒ The difference between choosing to wear just a hat and deciding to take an umbrella

❹ What is meant by visibility?

Ⓐ How much media coverage a celebrity gets

Ⓑ The amount of windshield not fogged up when you get in your car in the morning

Ⓒ The maximum horizontal distance at which prominent objects can be seen and identified by an observer of normal eyesight under existing atmospheric conditions

❺ **What is a front?**

Ⓐ The first part you see of a friendly person

Ⓑ A boundary between two different air masses

Ⓒ A lie set up to confuse people

❻ **What is a cold front?**

Ⓐ The leading or advancing edge of a cold air mass

Ⓑ The advancing troops in the Cold War

Ⓒ The first part you see of an unfriendly person

❼ **What causes a red sun?**

Ⓐ When you've been drinking too much

Ⓑ Increased length of the path traversed by its rays before the light reaches the observer

Ⓒ Increased length of the path home from the neighborhood bar

❽ **What causes a halo around the sun or moon?**

Ⓐ Pollution

Ⓑ The presence of cirriform clouds

Ⓒ When they've been really, really good

❾ **What causes sunburn?**

Ⓐ The sun—duh (½ point)

Ⓑ Stupidity

Ⓒ The ultraviolet or actinic rays of the sun

❿ **Who prepares the daily weather report?**

Ⓐ Monkeys

Ⓑ The U.S. Weather Bureau

Ⓒ Bookies down at the racetrack

Story Problems

❶ Janet goes to the store for a bottle of wine. On her way home, it begins to rain. If Janet walks at 0.5 mile per hour, approximately 20 raindrops per second will hit her head. If she runs at 1.0 mile per hour, 30 raindrops per hour will hit her head. Should she Ⓐ walk or Ⓑ run, for less rain to hit her head?

____

____

____

❷ Susie's umbrella has a radius of 1.5 feet and a circumference of 5 feet. The wind rips a pie-shaped piece out of ¼ of her umbrella. What are the measurements of the piece needed to patch Susie's umbrella?

____

____

____

❸ You have a hole in your ceiling approximately 3 inches in diameter. The bucket that you place under the drip can hold 2 gallons of rainwater. It is raining at the rate of 1 ounce per 5 minutes. How long will it take for the bucket to fill up?

____

____

____

Synonyms

❶ Rain
- Ⓐ Apocalypse
- Ⓑ Death
- Ⓒ Boredom

❷ Umbrella
- Ⓐ Phallus
- Ⓑ Bumbershoot
- Ⓒ Useless

❸ Sleet
- Ⓐ What the heck?
- Ⓑ What is this?
- Ⓒ Could the weather *get* any worse?

❹ Low-pressure system
- Ⓐ Bad
- Ⓑ Depression
- Ⓒ I'm moving to Florida

❺ Cloudburst
- Ⓐ Crying
- Ⓑ Moaning
- Ⓒ Telekinesis

❻ Jet Stream
- Ⓐ Trailer
- Ⓑ Screaming on airplane
- Ⓒ Rapid voiding

❼ Acclimatization
- Ⓐ Insane
- Ⓑ Impossible
- Ⓒ Move back to mom's house

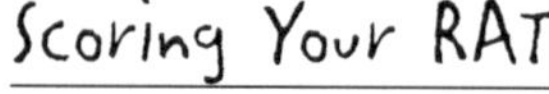

Congratulations on completing the RAT. Instead of a complex and mind-numbing scoring system that only breeds a mean-hearted, competitive spirit, we have come up with the following breakdown:

- If you cheated: You are ready for spring.
- If you had hot flashes at any time during this test: You can skip ahead to summer; you are way too ready for spring.
- If you cowered in a corner and soiled yourself at the thought of the RAT: Return to the beginning of this chapter.

April Fool's Day Pranks

Play these tricks on the un-emerged on April 1st—it's a hoot!

- Replace all of their shoes with flip-flops. Laugh as they trip all over the place.
- Replace all of their vodka with water. Giggle as they can't escape from their miserable, sober lives.
- Offer to become someone's buddy. Allow them to go out in public wearing spandex pants, a tank top, and white moon boots. Tell them, "You look great."
- Riddle their rubber raincoat with holes.
- Plant thousands of plastic flowers in their yard.
- Rig their umbrella to continuously play Milli Vanilli's "Blame It on the Rain" when it's opened.
- Teach their parrot to squawk, "Sunbreak!" during thunderstorms.
- Play videotapes of weather forecasts from August. Tell them it's tomorrow's forecast.

Northwest Weather Persona

Ace Deecee

Umbrella: No, likes the wet mullet look.

Winter gripe: Joint keeps going out in the rain.

Coping mechanism: Metallica.

Ace thinks the rain sucks, but it does make his acid-washed jeans appear even tighter, and that rocks.

May: Holy Bikini Season!

Average Low: 47°F
Average High: 66°F
Average Rainfall: 2"

Americans spend over $33 billion a year on diet foods, gadgets, and weight-loss services.

May

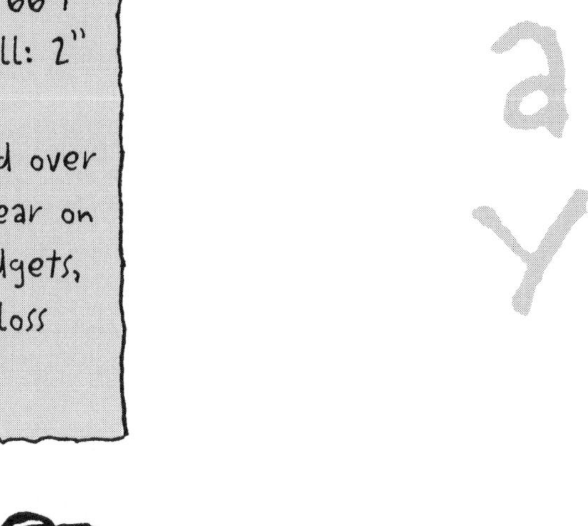

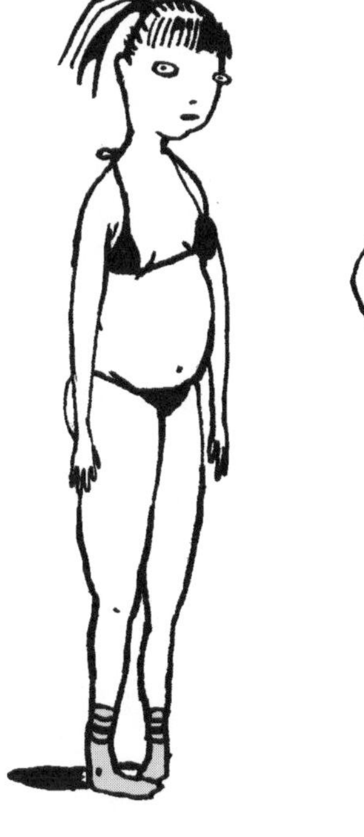

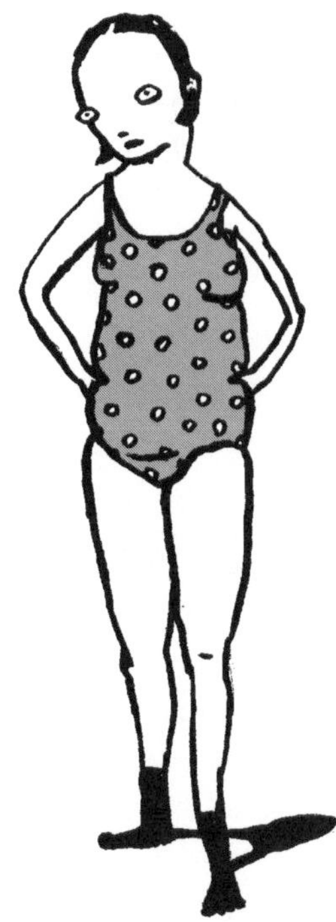

Even if you don't wear a bikini, you must prepare for bikini season. You won't be able to actually wear any type of bathing suit until August (unless you take a vacation to Mexico or Rio), but by starting in May, you'll have plenty of time to get ready—both mentally and physically.

Mental Preparation

Method 1: The Virtual You

❶ Make sure no one is home. Turn on your heater. Get the house up to 80 degrees.

❷ Dig through your closet and find your swimsuit, bikini, trunks, or whatever tight-fitting garment you wear to the beach.

❸ Put it on. No, take your clothes off *first,* then put it on.

❹ Get a camera and take several photos of yourself in the swimwear. Make sure to include a full-body shot.

❺ Develop the film and send your photo to www.efit.com, or if you are (or are dating) Web Fortran, scan the photo onto your computer.

❻ At efit, they will perform the patented process called the MORPHOVER. This means they will Photoshop 10–15 pounds of your chub right off your thighs, gut, and back. They will then send you a picture of the new you. Webbie can do the same thing on his computer.

7. Post this photo on your refrigerator. You now have a glowing example of yourself trying to achieve the impossible, media-driven standard of beauty.

Method 2: Positive Thinking

Think yourself thin!! For you lazy asses who actually believe in the power of the mind, try the following plan.

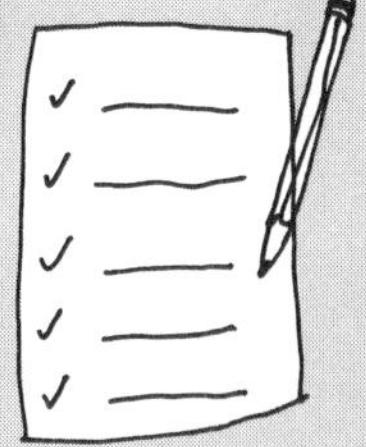

1. Write your goal in a journal.
2. Have a key word that you repeat to yourself when you're about to eat, say, an entire German chocolate cake. We recommend something sorta gross like "snot" or "Gene Wilder," but many have success with words like "thin" and "svelte."
3. Come up with a script to recite every morning to your reflection in the mirror, such as "I am getting thinner every day" or "I feel so fit and healthy." Try not to guffaw and heckle your image.
4. Dream exercise: Before you go to sleep at night, ask yourself a question. Maybe your brain will come up with a solution by the morning. We like: "How will my new bikini ever fit?" In the morning, don't be surprised if the word "Crisco" surfaces.

Method 3: Denial

1. Pretend it isn't actually getting warmer outside.
2. Manifest a fear of water, crowds, and beach towels.
3. Tell yourself you are allergic to the sun.
4. When someone says a word like "sand," "lake," or "flip-flops," act as if that person hasn't spoken at all.

Physical Preparation

Pet-xercise

Who wants to go jogging or for a walk when it's raining? Here are a bevy of exercises you don't need to leave the house to do! And best of all, your furry friends can help you out.

Underarms with Yertle

Stand with feet shoulder-width apart. Hold arms out to your sides at shoulder height, palms facing the ceiling. Have an assistant place a box turtle in each hand. Rotate arms in small circles counterclockwise. Now stop and rotate arms in small circles clockwise (this prevents the turtles from feeling sick to their stomach).

Sparkles Squat and Kiss

Place your cat Sparkles on the floor and stand above her. Slowly bend at the knees and gather kitty in your arms. Lift her off the floor by gently straightening your knees. Lower your head by bending your neck gently toward the cat. Kiss the cat on her cute little lips. Bend your knees and return the cat gently to the floor. Repeat until Sparkles leaves in a huff.

Leg Lifts with Lola

Sit in a chair. Alert your dog Lola that you have dog treats. Once Lola is standing before you, place your right leg between her hind legs and front legs, just under her stomach. Gently lift the pooch into the air. Give Lola a dog treat. Repeat using your left leg. Following the leg lifts, there will be a short upper-arm workout after Lola vomits.

Weather-Channel Workout

Turn on the news during the weather report and do the following exercises. By the time they get to the special-interest story, you'll be exhausted.

- ☐ Every time the weather forecaster says "rain," do five sit-ups.
- ☐ Every time the word "storm" is used, do five push-ups.
- ☐ If the forecaster says "clouds," do five pull-ups.
- ☐ If the forecaster says "blizzard," even in jest, jog in place for 15 minutes.
- ☐ If there's mention of a lightning storm, do six sets of jumping jacks.

Diet and Exercise Programs

At BRITE we've tested many well-known diet plans, and found they were ineffective. Popular plans like the Slim Fast diet encourage people to drink cans of a strange, chalky-flavored drink in lieu of breakfast and lunch, and enjoy a sensible meal for dinner. The Carbo Addict's diet requires the dieter to eat only protein for breakfast and lunch, and then a splurge meal including dessert for dinner. The problem lies in the "reward meal" concept—our test subjects celebrated very heartily indeed, with dinners featuring cupcakes by the dozen, whole pigs, and buckets of gravy. Instead, we recommend people make a few simple lifestyle changes to shave off those unwanted pounds.

The New Yorker's Diet Plan

Hey, those New Yorkers aren't pencil-thin just because they have to chase after subway trains! Begin by preparing your apartment or home to increase feelings of stress: Block off three-quarters of your living space to simulate a typical New Yorker's apartment; special-order some cockroaches and set them free in the kitchen and bathroom; play an audiotape loop featuring the sounds of ambulances, yelling, and honking. Then put yourself on a strict budget of $10 a day for food.

Day 1
Breakfast: Bagel and coffee.
Lunch: One slice of pizza.
Dinner: None, ran out of money.
Should feel a little anxious and claustrophobic, which decreases appetite.
Exercise option: Pace bedroom until late into the night.

Day 2
Breakfast: Coffee.
Lunch: One slice of pizza.
Dinner: Bagel.
The sight of the cockroaches scurrying about extinguishes any feelings of hunger.
Exercise option: Run around the apartment killing roaches. Don't worry—you will *never* kill them all.

Day 3
Breakfast: Coffee.
Lunch: Bagel.
Dinner: Work late, no dinner.
Exercise option: Have a friend simulate a mugging.

Diet Recap
Weight loss per week: 10 pounds.
Bikini rating: 9 (actually looking a bit gaunt).
Side effects: Can't sleep at night; edginess; frequent bursts of rage and feelings of helplessness.

A Hippie Weight-Loss Program

On the hippie program, you may buy food only with money acquired through the sale of hemp necklaces. You may not eat meat, and all food must be organic. Warning: Before beginning this weight-loss plan, you must assign a friend the task of taking you off the diet. Utilize a code word that will snap you out of your pot-induced daze.

Day 1
Breakfast: None.
Lunch: Apple acquired from a fellow hippie at a drum circle.
Dinner: Buckwheat noodles.
Sell five necklaces. Feel very mellow.
Exercise option: Wrestle with friendly dog.

Day 2
Breakfast: One joint.
Lunch: Several oat and carob cookies.
Dinner: Pint of soy milk, banana, and wheat germ.
Pot-induced midnight snack: 25 fruit-rollups.
Sell 10 necklaces. Think about changing name to Harvest.
Exercise option: Hacky Sack.

Day 3
Breakfast: Berries gathered from park.
Lunch: Barley soup.
Dinner: One joint and organic yogurt.
Pot-induced midnight snack: Two pints of Ben and Jerry's Cherry Garcia ice cream.
Sell 15 necklaces. Consider road trip to Santa Cruz.
Exercise option: Perform the whirling-dervish, "I'm-on-acid" hippie dance in the park.

Diet Recap
Weight loss per week: 5 pounds (would've lost more weight except for those chronic "munchies").
Bikini rating: 8.
Side effects: Can't remember name.

Martha Stewart's Regime

The ground rule for this program is that you must make everything you eat, with your own hands—no processed foods. And the food must look beautiful. There is a constant exercise element to this diet plan as well: tightening your larynx to speak in a "happy" voice and brushing bangs out of your eyes 20 times an hour.

Day 1
Breakfast: A few berries gathered fresh out of the garden.
Lunch: Skip, in order to milk a cow and make yogurt, and gather fresh honey from beehives.
Dinner: Yogurt spiked with garden berries and drizzled with farm-fresh honey.
Exercise option: Paint kitchen pink.

Day 2
Breakfast: Coffee made from beans gathered and roasted by hand.
Lunch: Skip, in order to make rose wreath centerpiece for table.
Dinner: After cooking rack of lamb for 20 guests, you're too tired to eat.
Exercise option: Iron and fold all linens.

Day 3
Breakfast: Hot cereal—mill all grains by hand.
Lunch: Raw dandelion greens, hand-gathered.
Dinner: Skip, in order to organize spice rack.
Exercise option: Replace all hand-dug dandelions with spring bulbs.

Diet Recap
Weight loss per week: 8 pounds.
Bikini rating: 10.
Side effects: Can't stop saying, "It's a good thing."

Buying a New Swimsuit

Now that you're all slim and healthy, you want to go buy a new bathing suit, right? Here are some Dos and Don'ts.

Macramé Bikini

Do: If you are a college freshman sorority girl.
Don't: If, while wearing the bikini, your body looks like a tied pot roast.

Au Naturel

Do: If it's nighttime or you're at a nude beach.
Don't: If you think you might run into your mother-in-law.

The Grandma

Do: If you're a senior citizen.
Don't: If you're trying to get a date or a tan.

Your Underwear

Do: If your undies are clean.
Don't: If your undies are see-through.

Speedo

Do: Only if you are a vacationing European.
Don't: If your feelings are hurt by people pointing and laughing.

Thong

Do: If you're going to Rio.
Don't: If your butt clenches when you hear the word "thong," and it won't ease up until you've had some fried chicken.

Who Is Fat?

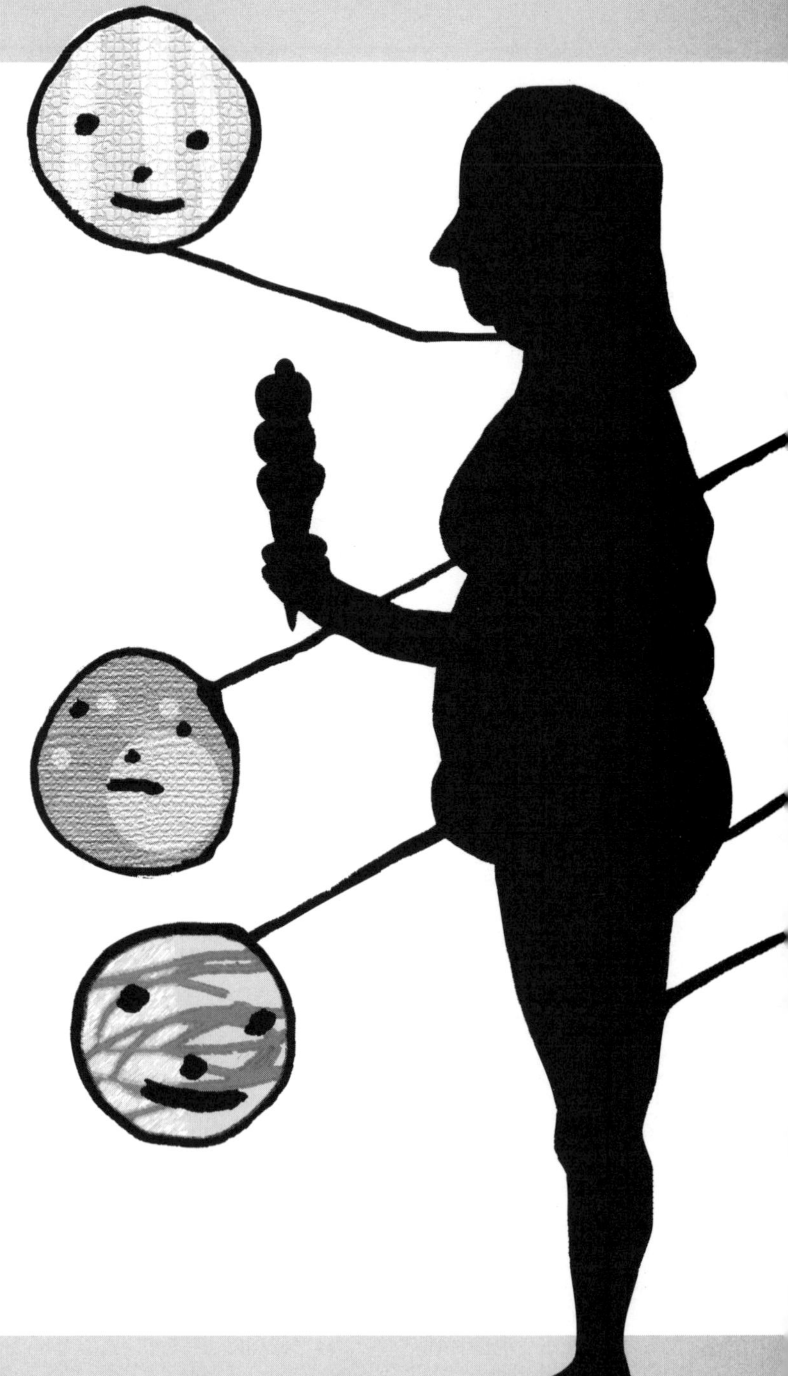

Fat is a wily character and shape shifter. It appears more often during the winter months, and it could be living on your body at this very moment. Here are a few of its aliases; watch for them when you are trying on your bathing suit.

Who Is Fat?

Flab

Last seen on arms and neck.
D.O.B.: When gravity was invented.
Length: 2–4 inches.
Weight added: Negligible, but weighs heavily on your body image.
Crime: Aggravated assault on your body tone.

Man Boobs

Frequents area formerly known as the pectoral region.
D.O.B.: After you quit college intramural weight-lifting league.
Length: 2–4 inches.
Weight added: 5 pounds.
Crime: Impersonating your Aunt Harriet's bosom.

Paunch, aka Potbelly

A rotund character that lingers in the stomach region.
D.O.B.: The day you reached the legal drinking age.
Height: 5–10 inches.
Weight added: 10–20 pounds.
Crime: Kidnapped your six-pack.

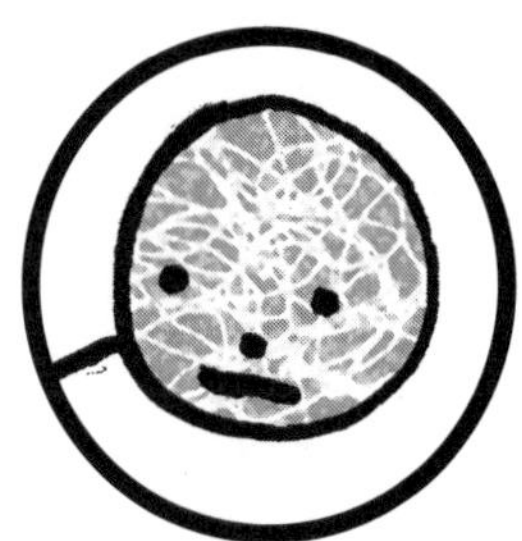

Chub, aka Back Fat

Hides out in the back area; comes out when you wear a tight shirt, bra, or strapless gown.
D.O.B.: Just after you finished that 15th drumstick.
Height: 3–5 inches.
Weight added: 2 pounds.
Crime: Gross misdemeanor.

Cellulite

Last seen on the backs of thighs.
D.O.B.: Thanksgiving.
Height: 1-inch pebbles.
Weight added: 5 pounds.
Crime: Murdered your ability to wear a bikini.

Saddle Bags

Known to hang out in the area where legs and butt converge.
D.O.B.: The day you turned 32.
Height: 3 inches.
Weight added: 5 pounds.
Crime: Stole your ability to stand in front of a mirror naked.

Northwest Weather Persona

Ice Cubes

Umbrella: Tommy, of course.

Winter gripe: Bass in his car stereo is distorted by humidity.

Coping mechanism: Wearing sunglasses.

Ice Cubes refuses to get out of his tricked-out Cadillac from the months of October through May. Why leave when there's a wet bar?

June: Killing Time Until the Sun Comes Out

Average Low: 52°F
Average High: 71°F
Average Rainfall: 1.5"

Average number of daylight hours in the Northwest in June per day: 15

June

Like many things in life—caviar, buffets, grad school—June can be a disappointment if you live in the Northwest. Where's the sun, the heat? Where are the scantily dressed babes? They are inside, like you, waiting for a sun break. But what'll you do while waiting? Eat an entire chocolate cake? Watch *Diff'rent Strokes* re-runs? BORING. How about trying your hand at something creative?

Make Your Own Wonder Bread Weather Station

Because idle hands are the devil's playthings, crafts are often relegated to the world of prisons and day cares. But when it's raining outside, this craft will stimulate the mind and erase boredom, and you can even predict the weather with it!

Materials Needed

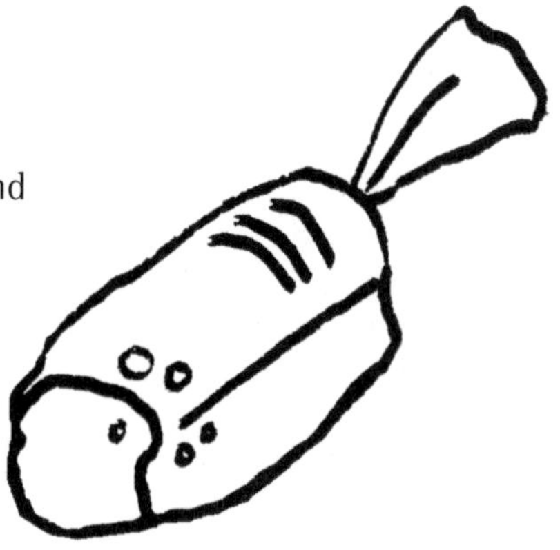

1 loaf Wonder Bread

1 wire coat hanger, unwound

1 package food coloring

Shellac

Glue

1 barometer

1 thermometer

Directional indicator: 1 pair of underwear

Steps

1. Remove Wonder Bread from bag. Take care to keep slices together so they retain loaf shape. Starting at the bottom, pierce loaf with unwound coat hanger. Crook it at one end, and allow 4 inches of wire to peek out of the top.

2. Pour food coloring randomly on loaf. Because Wonder bread is absorbent, it will drink the color right up. Try splatter patterns for a Jackson Pollock look, or polka dots. Let dry overnight.

3. Coat entire loaf with shellac. Glue barometer and thermometer to sides of loaf. Attach directional indicator to top. Place your Wonder Bread Weather Station outside, in an open area.

How to Use

Keep track of the changing atmospheric conditions by periodic checks on your new Wonder Bread Weather Station. If a storm's blowing in, so will your panties.

A severe weather front is moving in if:

- Your undies are blowing S to SE, and the barometer reads 29.80 and is falling rapidly.

- Your undies are blowing SE to NE, and the barometer reads 30.10 and is falling.

- Your undies are blowing S to E, and the barometer reads 29.80 or below and is falling.

A severe weather front with heavy rain and gale-force winds is on its way if:

- Your undies are blowing E to N, and the barometer reads 29.80 and is falling quickly.

Word Fun

A Poetry Primer

Some folks just aren't crafty. For them, poetry was created. Try your hand at a few of these, and remember: Write what you know.

Haiku

These are 17-syllable poems broken up into three lines, generally with a sequence of 5 syllables in the first line, 7 in the second, and 5 in the last. Haiku traditionally contains *akigo,* a word that describes nature.

Drop, drop, drip, drip, drip.
A rainbow in the puddle.
Caused by motor oil.

Sonnet

Meaning "little song" in Italian, a sonnet is a form of poetry created in 14th-century Italy. A popular form used by such writers as Shakespeare, a sonnet features 14 rhyming lines in an ababcdcdefefgg pattern, combined with iambic pentameter (10 syllables that fluctuate between stressed, then unstressed).

Ⓐ Shall I compare thee to a summer's day?

Ⓑ O, I wish I could, but can't remember–

Ⓐ Rough winter winds have blown my warmth away.

Ⓑ My darling, June may well be December.

Ⓒ Skies are gray and clouds do cover the sun.

Ⓓ Do I put on my bikini or wait?

Ⓒ Some cupcakes I did make, they're surely done.

Ⓓ Come over–will you be my hibermate?

Ⓔ Endless rain dampens my soul, and puddles

Ⓕ Outside will never hasten to the drain.

Ⓔ Ah, I have found you, come in for cuddles!

Ⓕ CCR said it best: "Who'll stop the rain?"

Ⓖ But the weatherman promised sun, you wail!

Ⓖ Tough shit, kid; he was simply telling a tale.

Limerick

Aha! Ribald poetry you can make up while drinking a pint of grog. Just use five lines with an aabba rhyming scheme.

Ⓐ There once was a man from Seattle.

Ⓐ Every winter he fought a battle.

Ⓑ He hated the rain.

Ⓑ And cried when it came.

Ⓐ Then one day he just went skedaddle.

Karaoke

Allow yourself to make up new lyrics to your favorite songs. Why go to a bar and embarrass yourself? Get your own karaoke system or simply hook up a mike to your stereo system. Those rainy-day doldrums will vanish once you start singing hits like Gloria Gaynor's "I Will Survive" or Pavement's "Summer Babe."

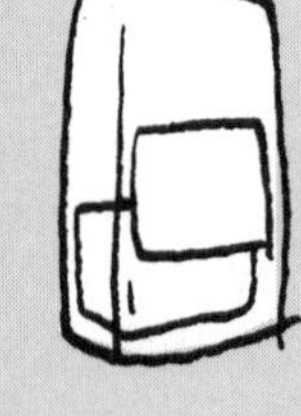

Weather-Changing Tips from the Ancients

Some people simply can't wait for the rain to stop and for summer to begin. For these people we have one word: shaman. Usually reserved for drought periods, shamans or medicine men are called upon to shift the weather. At BRITE we employ several shamans and they give the following advice:

To Bring Out the Sun/Stop the Ceaseless Rain

You must perform the following sun ceremony, borrowed (in an updated, modern form) from the Hottentots.

1. Gather 10 of your friends into your backyard.
2. Strip down to your underwear.
3. The oldest person in the group must purchase a six-pack of his or her favorite beer, from the corner deli. (Important: He or she must remain in underwear.)

4. When the elder brings the beer back, dig a hole and bury the beer in the ground.
5. Go inside and karaoke.
6. When the sun emerges, uncover the beer and let it go "free."
7. If successful, see pages 166-167.

Note: The shamans insist that one of the reasons it rains so often in the Northwest is because of the higher-than-usual number of rain sticks. Every time someone picks up one of those sticks and turns it upside down, that's a message to the gods asking them to make it rain. So, attention all you hippies: Lose those rain sticks, would you?

If You Want It to Rain

Who would actually want it to rain? Well, let's say you'd like to see your enemy's outdoor wedding ruined. Here's a fail-proof method, direct from the shaman's mouth.

1. Walk out to your backyard.
2. Climb a tree or pole.
3. Whisper rain sounds into the clouds' ears.

Note: The shaman also mentioned that when he washes his mule, the rains tend to come. So, try washing your mule.

To Stop Ceaseless Wind

Our elders used to think strong winds were demons that needed to be fought. They would wage war against the wind, throwing spears and hurling stones at it. We know better than that now and suggest these steps to calm strong winds:

1. Simply go outside.
2. Tell the wind to meet you at the bowling alley for a winner take-all tournament.
3. When the wind arrives at the bowling alley, slip a mickey into its Budweiser.

Is That the Sun?

If the sun does happen to peek out, take the following steps.

- ☐ Don't panic.
- ☐ Check again to make sure the sun is actually out.
- ☐ Cautiously put on flip-flops.
- ☐ Put on sunglasses (that sun can really burn the ol' eye-balls).
- ☐ Walk outside.
- ☐ Lick a finger and put it up to the sky. If your finger feels cold, go back inside. It will begin to rain in approximately 2 hours. If your finger feels warmish, continue on.
- ☐ Immediately strip down into your skimpiest clothes.
- ☐ If you have a convertible, put the roof down. If not, saw your car roof off.

- ☐ Slather your body with sunscreen rated SPF 24.
- ☐ Buy a large beverage with a straw. Drive around and honk at everyone.
- ☐ Drive to the house of each of your friends. Ask them if they are going to have a barbecue. If they're not, tell them you are having a barbecue.
- ☐ Buy a whole pig. Roast it Hawaiian-style in the backyard (just dig a trench, put the pig in it, and cover with coals). Do erect a huge tarp in case it does rain.
- ☐ Go back to the grocery store. Buy out the entire beer section.
- ☐ Eat until you can hardly move. Stay out until your sunscreen has worn out, and you develop a sunburn as red as a baboon's bottom.
- ☐ Complain.
- ☐ Repeat the next day, weather permitting.

Weather-Predicting Tips

A long, long time ago, there was this guy named Theophrastus who, besides being friends with Aristotle, also came up with a bunch of signs for predicting short-term changes in the weather—things like "When the ox licks his forehoof, it will rain." Following his method of inquiry, folk began predicting short-term weather changes based on their observations. Here are a few of the more accurate ones:

- A red sky at dawn means a storm is blowing in, a red sky at night is a "sailor's delight" because it means the weather will probably be clear the next morning.
- Pour strong coffee into a cup to form some bubbles. Stir the coffee and observe the bubbles. If the bubbles scatter and then form toward the center of the cup, the weather will be fair. If they head toward the side of the cup, it might rain soon.
- Take a moment to scope out the hairdos around you. If you notice everyone's hair is looking very straight and tamed, the day will be dry. If people's hair seems out of control, frizzy, and generally bouffant, it'll be a wet day.
- In the days when they used leeches for bloodletting, physicians noticed that the leeches they kept in big glass jars would lie on the bottom of the jar during calm weather, but would get antsy just before a big storm. The more riled up, the stronger the storm. The only question is: Where the hell do you buy leeches?

June Activity Book

What's Different?

Most people look a little different in the summer compared to the winter. Can you find the 7 changes?

During Winter | During Summer

Answers: Wearing flip-flops, not boots. Carrying a picnic basket. No hairy winter legs. No booze bottle. No bags under eyes. No stinky winter hat. Flowers in hair.

Bad Lib

Fill in the missing information and create your personalized story about making it through the Northwest rainy season. Tip: Don't read it as you fill in the blanks, and use dirty words—that makes it so much funnier!

Ima Toorich was sick of the weather in the Northwest. Since she has tons of money, she ________ (adverb) bought a(n) ________ (noun #1) from ________ (famous person #1). Ima ________ (past-tense verb) it every day. On the weekends, she sleeps with ________ (funny name), the name she gave ________ 's (famous person #1) former ________ (noun #1). However, during a ________ (weather event), Ima discovered that ________ (famous music group) has a ________ (adjective) ________ (noun #1), so she stole it. Now Ima has two ________ (plural noun #1), and she's happier than a ________ (barnyard animal) in ________ (synonym for excrement).

Mix and Match

Can you match the following clothing items to the feeling that wearing it engenders? Draw a line to match the two columns.

Clothing Item	Feeling
❶ Wool sweater	Ⓐ Yuppies rule!
❷ Cowboy boots	Ⓑ Bike messengers are badasses.
❸ Rain poncho	Ⓒ I'm itchy.
❹ Gore-Tex	Ⓓ I'm wearing a garbage bag.
❺ Hoody	Ⓔ Gotta cigarette?
❻ Acid-washed jean jacket	Ⓕ I love Dwight Yoakam.
❼ Shorts in winter	Ⓖ I'm warm, but I'm still an asshole.
❽ Fur coat	Ⓗ I want to look cool at Monster Trucks this weekend.
❾ Leather	Ⓘ I'm *so* punk rawk.

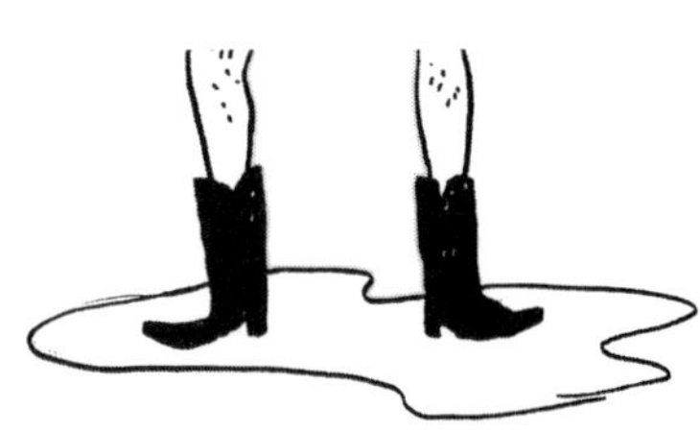

Answers: ❶ c; ❷ f; ❸ d; ❹ a; ❺ i; ❻ h; ❼ b; ❽ g; ❾ e

Word Scavenger Hunt

Throughout this book we've used some pretty interesting words. Can you find what page each of these appear on?

Ⓐ ear hole
Ⓑ jim-dandy
Ⓒ bouffant
Ⓓ hair spray
Ⓔ glowworm
Ⓕ bed head
Ⓖ loogies
Ⓗ rain sticks
Ⓘ skedaddle
Ⓙ striptease

Answers: Ⓐ pg 36; Ⓑ pg 39; Ⓒ pg 168; Ⓓ pg 24; Ⓔ pg 62; Ⓕ pg 118; Ⓖ pg 27; Ⓗ pg 164; Ⓘ pg 162; Ⓙ pg 26

Summer Drinking

Bored with your usual summer drink? Here are some suggestions to spice things up.

Ye Olde English with a Touch of Class

Buy one 40-ounce malt liquor of your choice.
Place 40-ouncer in champagne chiller filled with ice for 15 minutes.
Pour small amounts of malt liquor into small, cold cups.
Savor that flavor!

Junkie Watermelon

Buy a thin, narrow watermelon.
Dress watermelon up in shabby clothes.
Fill needles with vodka tinted with red food coloring.
Give the junkie watermelon his "fix," over and over again.
Consume junkie watermelon when he nods out.

Siberian Surprise

Buy a block of ice.
Sit on it.
Drink shot after shot of vodka.

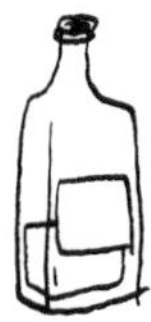

Airplane Bottle Roulette

Go to the liquor store, and purchase 10 airplane bottles of your favorite kinds of alcohol.
Place bottles on a lazy Susan on your kitchen table.
Spin the lazy Susan. When the lazy Susan stops spinning, drink the bottle closest to you.

Northwest Weather Persona

Skippy College

Umbrella: Yes; school colors!

Winter gripe: Sleeping in and missing class.

Coping mechanism: Speed.

Skip must avoid taking classes like "The Existential Crisis in the Novel" during winter quarter and opt for "Rocks for Jocks" instead.

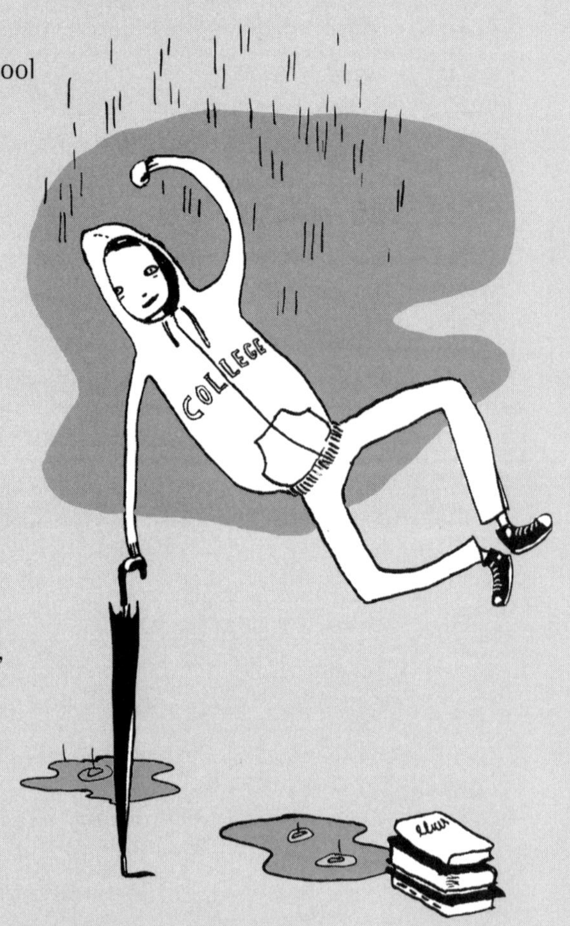

July & August: The Delirious, Short Northwest Summer

Average Low:
A happy 56°F
Average High: 77°F
Average Rainfall:
A happy 1"

Number of times this book used the word "ass": 1

JULY & August

100 Reasons to Be Happy

Happy happy basil happy happy ice cream happy sand happy happy sunlight happy happy barbecues happy happy cold beer happy outdoor karaoke happy happy sunscreen happy happy flip-flops happy happy volleyball happy happy outdoor sex happy happy happy hammocks happy warm breezes happy swimming happy sailing happy happy gardens happy happy smell of cut grass happy happy happy sunglasses happy Slip 'n Slide happy happy Fourth of July happy happy bonfires happy fresh tomatoes happy smell of tanning lotion happy happy slushies happy happy lots of skin exposed happy happy happy happy barefeet happy happy shorts happy frisbee happy water skiing happy happy smell of charcoal fluid happy happy grilled steaks happy happy convertible happy tank tops happy coleslaw happy happy burgers happy happy lemonade happy happy gin and tonic happy happy watermelon happy happy freckles happy happy happy crushed ice happy happy birdies happy happy roses happy happy porch sitting happy happy kites happy happy happy happy happy happy happy naked happy happy happy happy tire swing happy happy happy floppy hat happy happy happy cutoffs happy happy happy happy happy dappled shadows happy happy happy happy road trip happy happy happy camping happy happy happy happy happy carnival happy happy happy blackberries happy happy happy happy picnic happy happy happy

happy happy cruising happy happy happy radio happy happy tennis happy happy swan dive happy happy happy happy sundress happy happy sidewalk cafe happy happy happy blue sky happy happy happy happy sunflower happy strappy sandals happy happy rootbeer float happy happy ponytail happy happy happy happy waterguns happy happy happy sprinklers happy happy drive-ins happy happy happy cabin happy happy bumblebee happy hummingbirds happy happy trampoline happy happy kiddy pool happy happy happy sand sculpture happy happy sweaty bodies happy low-rider bicycles happy happy black-eyed susans happy happy happy skipping rocks happy happy iced tea happy happy snow cones happy happy happy corn-on-the-cob happy watermelon seed spitting contests happy happy happy naked water skiing happy happy beach bonfires happy happy happy peaches happy happy cherries happy happy happy strawberries with sour cream and brown sugar happy happy outdoor showers happy wild berry California coolers happy happy star-gazing happy happy happy weenie roast happy happy campfire songs happy blueberries happy motorcycle riding happy happy convertibles happy happy horror movies at the drive-in happy happy happy warm mornings happy happy happy happy dew on grass happy happy dog park happy happy car washing happy happy warm hose water happy happy belly-button sweat pools.

Northwest Weather Persona

R.E. Inn

Umbrella: Would Krakauer use an umbrella? No.

Biggest winter gripe: Hard to decide which of his five Gortex jackets to wear.

Coping mechanism: Having sex in a snow cave built with his own hands.

R.E. loves the Northwest weather. He accepts with vigor the challenge of keeping dry and buys product after product to guarantee protection from the elements. Job at dot.com company essential to updating gear.

Books

Aromatherapy: The Complete Guide to Plant and Flower Essences for Health and Beauty. Daniele Ryman. New York: Bantam Books, 1991.

The Complete Book of Survival. Rainer Stahlberg. New York: Barricade Books, 1998.

Illness as Metaphor. Susan Sontag. New York: Farrar, Straus, and Giroux, 1977.

1001 Weather Questions Answered. Frank Forrester. New York: Dover, 1982.

Rains All the Time: A Connoisseur's History of Weather in the Pacific Northwest. David Laskin. Seattle: Sasquatch Books, 1997.

Weather Forecasting. Michael Hodgson. Old Saybrook, Conn.: Globe Pequot, 1992.

Winter Blues: Seasonal Affective Disorder. Norman Rosenthal. New York: Guilford Press, 1993.

Suggested Web Sites

- www.storm-track.com
  For lunatics. They even have their own magazine.
- www.spc.noaa.gov
  The storm prediction center. Cool photos of tornados and stuff.
- www.nws.noaa.gov/
  The National Weather Service. Features ultrasound-looking satellite imagery. (Um, the Pacific Northwest looks like it has a tumor!)
- www.wrcc.dri.edu/
  For anyone living in the West. The Western Regional Climate Center has tons of climate information for hundreds of cities. Find out what the average rainfall is in Eugene! The inches of snow in Astoria! Warning: All those statistics and charts can get a bit depressing.
- www.sltbr.org
  The Society for Light Treatment and Biological Rhythms. Join the club! Get updates!
- www.psychiatry.ubc.ca/mood/md_sad.html
  Don't be scared of the UBC's use of the word "Mood Disorder."
- www.sunnexbiotech.com/
  Out of Winnipeg, Canada. Some weird-looking light boxes offered here. It's worth a try . . .
- www.nu-light.com/
  Company that sells light therapy boxes.
- www.lighttherapyproducts.com/
  Why do all of these have a sun illustration?
- www.phatcycles.com/chopper.html
  Er...Check out those choppers! Yee-haw!!

Glossary of Terms*

*all entries are to be read in the voice of Bill Gates/Don King/ or Rocky Balboa

Afro: the finest of the recommended hairdos for conserving warmth

Barbecue Buddy: eating partner who will order you an extra side of yams

Beef Jerky Jim-dandy: eating partner who will buy you a can of "jerky chew"

Bikini: abstract concept that embodies summer

Body heat index: ultra-scientific numerical placeholder that defines "hot potential" in hibermates

BRITE: Beyond Rain and Ignorance Teaching Establishment

Butter: food item and type of lip protection

California cooler: summer beverage

Cellulite: the most insidious of the many kinds of fat that may be found on a winter body

Chub: one of the cutest of many kinds of fat that may be found on a winter body

Coffee: beverage that must be stockpiled

Cough syrup: both medicine and hallucinogen

Dawn simulator: expensive alarm clock

Decaf: beverage for the dimwitted

Decongestant: reduces snot; when paired with booze, serves as muscle relaxant

Dim Sum Delight: eating partner who will order you just one more plate of dumplings filled with questionable pork products

Ding Dongs: source of inspiration for winter-blues sufferers worldwide

Doldrums: sexual boredom

Doughnut Doppelganger: eating partner who will not blink twice when you suggest you each order a dozen

Expectorant: makes you cough up phlegm; can also be used to make wonderful beaded necklaces

Farrah Fawcett: one of the recommended hairdos that conserves warmth and, by virtue of aerosol cans, simultaneously increases global warming

Flab: one of many kinds of fat that may be found on a winter body

Flip-flops: dangerous footwear, to be worn only in the summer (after much practice)

Freezer-case Friend: eating partner who will don extra layers of clothing so that you may linger longer in the freezer section of your grocery store

Fried-chicken Chum: eating partner who will say, "What! Only one chicken for each of us?!"

Haiku: type of poem that will bring tears of joy to your eyes

Hibermate: person who you use, during winter months usually, only for their body heat

Hogan's Heroes: television show that, when viewed in the afternoon, can kill the will to live

Karaoke: weather predictor; activity of the gods

Light visor: ugly-maker

Lightbox: expensive refrigerator lights

Man boobs: one of the funniest of many kinds of fat that may be found on a winter body

M.A.S.H.: television show that can mentally cripple you

Mohawk: hair don't

Moustache: hair don't

Mullet: hairdo that retains heat in the critical neck region

P.O.W.: Prisoner of Weather

Pagan party: Christians bugging you? Jews too? Go pagan

Pigtails: hipster hair don't du jour

Polar fleece: the polyester pantsuit of the 1990s

Rain sticks: Why, I ask you? Why?

RAT: Re-emergence Aptitude Test

Re-emergence: only for the brave

Ritalin: med to get from a medical professional or your 8-year-old cousin

Saddle bags: one of many kinds of fat that may be found on a winter body

Sinusitis: opportunity to acquire prescription meds

Slip 'n' Slide: activity of the summer gods

Spring fever: debilitating condition

Tequiza: alcoholic beverage that defies logic

Tinctures: yucky herbs soaking in yummy alcohol

Warma Sutra: positions for warmth

Weather Personas: profiles of Northwestern personalities that appear throughout this book

Weather warrior: person who knows how to stockpile booze

Weather wary: person who sort of knows how to stockpile booze

Weather wimp: person who doesn't know what booze is

Wellbutin: orgasmic pharmie

Winter soul: eat food, fool!